Buckley vs. Vidal
The Historic 1968 ABC News Debates

DEVAULT-GRAVES
DIGITAL EDITIONS
www.devault-gravesagency.com
Memphis, Tennessee

DEVAULT-GRAVES DIGITAL EDITIONS
An imprint of The Devault-Graves Agency, LLC.
2197 Cowden Ave.
Memphis, Tennessee 38104

Print Edition ISBN: 978-1-942531-12-8
Ebook ISBN: 978-1-942531-11-1

Cover design: Martina Voriskova
Title page design: Martina Voriskova
Layout: Patrick Alley

**DEVAULT-GRAVES
DIGITAL EDITIONS**
www.devault-gravesagency.com

Table of Contents

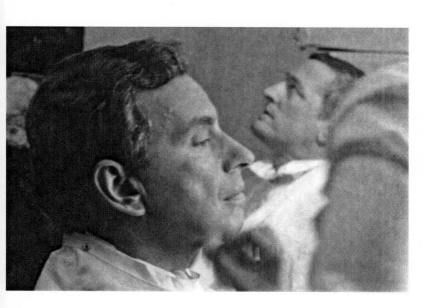

INTRODUCTION
by Robert Gordon

THEY CAME LOADED FOR bear. William F. Buckley Jr. and
Gore Vidal, representing the political poles in America, sat in
front of the ABC News cameras in 1968 and, though hired
to discuss the events of each party's political conventions and
their path toward their presidential tickets, these men each
arrived with the intention of taking down the other. For the
good of the nation.

During the summer 1968 Republican and Democratic
conventions, the United States was in turmoil, the chasm
between youth culture and the establishment widening as
the war in Vietnam dragged on, killing kids, killing civilians,
killing hope. In March of that year, two weeks after the My Lai
Massacre, President Lyndon Johnson announced he would
not seek reelection. Dr. Martin Luther King Jr. was assassinated in April. Bobby Kennedy was assassinated two months
later. Riots raged across the United States, in cities large and
small. Major publications gave serious consideration to the
possibility of a new U.S. civil war.

Unlike now, the conventions were not a stage play with
the outcomes decided. In 1968, neither party went in with a
clear candidate. Actual politics would be conducted.

For the previous several conventions, the three television
networks had made it their journalistic duty to cover the pro-
ceedings "gavel-to-gavel," meaning from late afternoon until
whenever business was concluded, usually before midnight,

but, if there were a floor fight, well into the night.

Of the three networks — there were only three then, plus the precursor to PBS — ABC was a distant third. It had been founded later, was less funded, had fewer affiliates. It had neither the resources nor the personalities to draw viewership and, in '68, the ABC network chiefs decided they couldn't afford gavel-to-gavel coverage. It wasn't that live coverage was expensive; rather, they needed the income that their prime-time programming would generate. While NBC and CBS would broadcast political speeches, ABC offered instead *The Flying Nun, Bewitched, Batman,* and *Land of the Giants* (giving a new meaning to TV as escapism). Then, after its regular nightly news, ABC would offer 90 minutes of what it termed "unconventional convention coverage," a five-segment nightly summation of the day. They'd open with a synopsis of the day's events and close with an update. In between was "Corre-spondents' Caucus," a roundtable discussion from the leading ABC reporters; "Closeup," an in-depth analysis of the day's major events, and "A Second Look," which featured Buckley and Vidal and was described in a press release: "William F. Buckley Jr. and Gore Vidal will 'discuss,' in their usually irreverent fashion, the men and issues. Astute and articulate observers of the political scene, the conservative Buckley and outspoken liberal Vidal are expected to disagree occasionally."

ABC was ridiculed by news organizations from all media for forsaking its journalistic responsibility, but the results of their desperate measure surprised everyone.

Both Buckley and Vidal had already developed large public personae, including a renowned dislike for each other.

Their first confrontation had been in print in 1961, a series of Associated Press columns, each presenting opposing sides on current affairs. Then in 1962 Vidal, already a favorite guest of TV talk show host Jack Paar, made fun of Buckley and *National Review* for rejecting Pope John XXIII's encyclical *Mater et Magistra*, which called on Catholics to embrace social progress. Buckley learned of this televised insult as he was departing the country and he left a telegram with his office to send to Paar that, according to Buckley, included the line: PLEASE INFORM GORE VIDAL THAT NEITHER I NOR MY FAMILY IS DISPOSED TO RECEIVE LESSONS IN MORALITY FROM A PINK QUEER. His office did not send it and instead Buckley demanded time for a response, garnering his first national TV appearance. There he surprised Paar by speaking intelligently and precisely from a conservative viewpoint when Paar was expecting the prejudiced and crude talk associated with the John Birch Society, the group that had long emblematized the political right. But Buckley had been actively re-branding the conservatives, distancing the movement from what he called "the kooks and the anti-Semites," positioning himself as a spokesman for a thoughtful, reasoned political stance. Buckley handled himself well on television and, like Vidal, understood the power of the medium to reach into broad swaths of America personally, with a message undiluted.

Despite political differences, the two men seemed cut from the same cloth: their mid-Atlantic speaking accents were haughty, their demeanors were aloof, they exuded breeding and education. However, for each, these airs had been cultured; they were not born into the Eastern establishment, and didn't have the usual New England prep school backgrounds (though each did attend elite academies, Buckley at Andover and Vidal at Exeter). Vidal came from Oklahoma and Tennessee stock and was raised in the U.S. Senate where his blind grandfather served, developing a political education by reading aloud to him the Congressional Record and other necessary documents. Buckley's family was wealthy, but nouveau, their Catholicism keeping them outside the WASPish circle of their neighboring Connecticut bluebloods. Tutored from an early age, Buckley went on to Yale while Vidal opted not to pursue college — each angling for his own route of attack on the culture's dominant forces. Vidal published his first book in 1946 but became an enfant terrible with *The City and the Pillar* in 1948, a novel that dealt unapologetically and sympathetically with a homosexual protagonist. Buckley published his first book three years later, *God and Man at Yale*, a controversial attack on an institution that he proclaimed was leaning too far left, promulgating communism, and attacking religion. Their positions staked, we can look back and see these polar opposites being slowly drawn toward each other.

As outsiders with atypical establishmentarian backgrounds, they were comfortable moving to television at a time when the boob tube was still disparaged as déclassé. On September 23, 1962, they appeared together on the David Susskind program, a tete-a-tete that proved them equally matched for wit, though polarized in world views. Apparently neither felt like they'd completed what they set out to do at that meeting and they appeared again with Susskind on July 15, 1964 from the San Francisco Republican National Convention. There, the sparring continued, an undercurrent of loathing gradually surfacing, and afterward Buckley informed Vidal he wanted to never see him again, the rare statement from Buckley with which Vidal could agree.

Enter ABC and 1968. As the press release reveals, ABC knew that bringing the two together could create friction and that the sparks could attract more viewers. In fact, when Buckley was hired, they asked him, perhaps slyly, whom he'd like as an opponent from the liberal side, and then asked him for names he'd prefer not to debate. Buckley, as he later recounted in *Esquire*, said that as a matter of principle he'd not debate a communist, and also not Gore Vidal "because I had had unpleasant experiences with him in the past and did not trust him." Vidal, who also claims he was hired first, says he asked not to face Buckley because he didn't want to lend him any credibility or create opportunity for him to spread his message. Nonetheless, each assented when he learned who his opponent would be, drawn no doubt by the power of the national audience he'd have and also, significantly, by the $10,000 fee (approximately $70,000 in 2015 currency). Their tasks also included filming commentaries inserted into the newscasts prior to the conventions and appearing in November on election night.

Coverage began two days prior to each convention. Within minutes of their first conversation, these high-minded individuals took the low road. After Vidal contemns the Republicans as the party of greed, Buckley turns personal, assaulting Vidal and his most recent novel, *Myra Breckinridge,* which Vidal once described as about "a man who becomes a woman who becomes a man" — scandalous for its time and quickly a bestseller. Though Buckley was first in shifting from the political to the personal, Vidal had come prepared to do just that, having hired researchers to create a dossier on Buckley and pre-scripting pages of insults to hurl at his opponent. (My favorite is describing Buckley as "the Marie Antoinette of the right-wing.") Buckley, who had opened a dossier on Vidal in 1965, makes frequent insinuations about Vidal's homosexuality, saying in the first debate, "We know your tendency is to be feline, Mr. Vidal."

These dialogues, ostensibly political commentary, wound up being much more personal because each saw in the other, as Buckley biographer Sam Tanenhaus has said, "a kind of exaggerated image of his own anxious version of himself." *Like a dark funhouse mirror, what if the public sees me as I see my opponent?* If Buckley reviled Vidal's pansexuality as a perversity that would dissolve the stability of God, country, and family, Vidal saw Buckley as a shill for corporate greed whose erudite rhetoric cloaked the mechanisms of exploitation and impoverishment. More than morally or ideologically offensive, each perceived his opponent as a beacon for danger, a determined, imminent threat intent on taking down the nation.

While Buckley's gay-baiting is undeniable throughout these encounters, his history suggests that he was comfortable among gay men. Buckley and his wife Patricia entertained many gays at their New York and Connecticut homes; Patricia was a fundraiser for the Metropolitan Museum of Art, and many of their art-world friends were homosexual. Nonetheless, he focused on Vidal's homosexuality as the avenue to express his animus.

However much these attacks anticipate the political television of today, they are also strikingly different. The sheer time allotted — fifteen uninterrupted minutes — is so unlike TV now, when commercial breaks are four or seven minutes apart, and when the moderator also wants to be a prominent personality. Howard K. Smith, the network's host, is rarely seen, much less heard, and his directives are acknowledged but often dismissed. (Smith's very first question is redirected by Buckley, who casually replies, "I think what you really mean to ask me . . . ") And though both commentators wear earpieces it's clear that there's no producer shouting to them, "Get off this topic, the viewer numbers are going down." Ask any commentator today about what they hear in their ear and you get a quick lesson in how televised political commentary is driven not by issues but by viewer responses, by ratings, by producers with their eyes on graphs of instant audience reactions.

Not unlike the way exposure to the natural elements destroys old paper and paintings, the national camera and its bright lights serve to degrade wit, erudition, and commitment to political thought. Before these debates were over — in the penultimate meeting, as if scripted by a Hollywood writer — Buckley and Vidal were reduced to schoolyard name-calling, an ugly ad hominem attack that had been brewing for years, that night after night the klieg lights had warmed until ready to serve. And even after returning for the final show, when they'd clearly been chastened, each answering the moderator and then sitting quietly while the other did the same, when their body language was like two inverted parentheses, each keeping as much of himself as far from the other as physically possible — Buckley and Vidal were not done with each other. *Esquire* magazine, a bastion of the American essay, invited Buckley to examine the course of events, leading to a recapitulation of the aggrievement that didn't terminate it but rather perpetuated it, with Buckley acknowledging his bad behavior and concluding, "I herewith apologize to Gore Vidal," though he'd just spent 10,000 words mostly justifying what he'd done. The attack couched as self-examination fooled no one, least of all Vidal, who seized the opportunity to submit his own take in the same magazine's pages the following month. Unlike Buckley's "On Experiencing Gore Vidal," Vidal made no bones about his angle, titling his piece, "A Distasteful Encounter with William F. Buckley Jr." Vidal focused on a decades-old Buckley family incident when several of Buckley's siblings vandalized and defaced a church in their town because they'd heard their father, William F. Buckley Sr., an avowed anti-Semite, condemn the preacher's wife, who'd sold property in their hometown to Jews. Bill Jr. was not involved in the incident, a fact not easily surmised from Vidal's piece. That implication, along with insinuations about Buckley's sexual proclivities, led to a lawsuit by Buckley against Vidal and against *Esquire*, then to a countersuit from Vidal, and further to the public digging at each other on TV talk shows and in print interviews. The angling for the upper hand, the attempts to finally destroy the other, dragged on for three years until finally *Esquire* found the legal fees no longer sustainable and settled with Buckley in a way that brought everything to a close. There was no victory over Vidal, though that did not stop Buckley from quickly declaring one, a move that assured their mutual and unending enmity.

After the 1968 conventions, the networks that ridiculed ABC adopted its format; none has presented gavel-to-gavel coverage since. And the ratings increase wrought by the increasingly acrimonious debates made the other networks arch their eyebrows and consider the revenue that argument afforded. By the 1970s, CBS instituted "Point-Counterpoint" on its *60 Minutes* news magazine, pairing two opposing views in short segments. The sides delivered prepared remarks and didn't engage, but the stark opposition was foregrounded and audiences liked to see the sly imprecations. (*Saturday Night Live* famously satirized the segment with Dan Aykroyd and Jane Curtin.) Television formatting evolved toward shorter segments with increasingly vociferous moderators, producing more fireworks more frequently, ultimately forsaking the content — a professional wrestling match where success is judged by how angry or excited the audience becomes. Where Buckley and Vidal were a forest fire fueled by acres of old wood, today we surf channels between pieces of flash paper exploding — big flames, no content.

Provocation has replaced vocation. News has devolved to the ready quip, the soundbite that makes possible headline news that fosters the tweet: the whole story in 140 characters. The environment changed, making extinct the public intellectual and breeding the attractive, striking, and exuberant talking head who fearlessly ignores interesting and challenging conversation to always drive home the talking point. Buckley and Vidal meander and tarry, gamboling in their command of history, politics, economics, and literature, spending their five-dollar words like they're at a penny slot machine. When was the last time you heard Pericles quoted on TV, or any philosopher ancient or modern? TV's appeal to the lowest common denominator may not be news, but seeing and hearing these debates nearly five decades after they occurred is a stark and harsh reminder of how far we've fallen.

In 2010, Memphis writer and professor Tom Graves (also publisher of this book) shared a bootleg copy of the debates with me. I immediately wanted to make a documentary film built around them and set about doing so with my film partner Morgan Neville and with Tom. The resulting *Best of Enemies* has served to jolt audiences the way the debates jolted us. Time and again it has been introduced with the word "delicious," though that word is nowhere in the movie or our press materials; it indicates the hunger Americans have for intellectual rigor, even if the serving in these debates is only an appetizer. Televised political commentary, like fast food, is filling but it does not nourish. Audiences are welcoming the opportunity to view people committed to considered, deliberate thought. To grow as a nation, to flourish as a republic, we need our fourth estate to strengthen us, not fatten us.

I have a naïve hope for the documentary. In the vast and shallow mediascape in which we live, when variations of a single idea fill hour after hour on network after network, such that the hundreds of channels seem to offer less variety than the three networks did those many years ago, there must be a failing network that will look around and ask itself, Before we fold entirely, is there an audience not yet being served for whom we could create programming? A format that allows deep discussion, that lets educated people speak without driving them always to the day's most salacious doings, that doesn't shy from vehement disagreement but also doesn't guarantee it — would people want to watch that?

I remember how radio station WDIA, in the late 1940s, found that Memphis, Tennessee didn't need a sixth spot on the dial like all the other five, and before going under, they took a wild shot and began programming 15 minutes a day for African-Americans. In short order, WDIA grew to become the first station in the country with an all-black on-air line up, and it jumped from last place to #2 and then led the market.

It's true that today we are hard put to make a list of public intellectuals who might fill such a network. The venues that used to incubate them are gone. But they are out there, in universities, as occasional guests on radio and TV talk shows where their thoughts are cut off and debased. Give them some air time and the ethos will grow, the mighty will rise to the occasion.

We need public intellectuals to help us understand our times. Otherwise, we are subject to the Internet, where authority has been replaced by graphics — if it looks real it must be real, and where search engines create echo chambers of opinion. That is, we each may search Google, but the responses to "Obama" or "healthcare" or "same-sex marriage" will be different, can be antithetical, based upon what the search engine has gleaned are the askers' individual viewpoints. Lies and fictions are presented as truths by bloggers and websites (search engines do not check facts, only seek words), allowing contradictory statements to co-exist when both can't be true. In 1946, in the days after World War II, presidential advisor Bernard Baruch said, "Every man has a right to his own opinion, but no man has a right to be wrong in his facts." Variations have been uttered by U.S. Secretary of Defense James R. Schlesinger, U.S. Senator Daniel Patrick Moynihan, and others. Today this seemingly indisputable truth no longer holds. Propaganda is indistinguishable from fact and we find ourselves living in the frightening pages of a George Orwell novel.

The takeaway from these debates has spawned a bastard progeny of vacuity. But what is delicious is not the shouting that came near the culmination of the Buckley-Vidal debates, but the stroll down the path that led to it. These men bring resources to the table, knowledge and ideas — along with their sharp knives. Read on, dive in, luxuriate in these words, these battles and contretemps. Laugh with the witty retorts and let William Buckley and Gore Vidal fuel our appetites for real dialogue in this great nation.

— Robert Gordon
Producer/Director (with Morgan Neville)
of *Best of Enemies*

The Republican National Convention, 1968
Miami Beach, Florida

Debate One — Republican Convention
Saturday, August 3, 1968
Miami Beach, Florida
(Two days prior to convention)

Editor's Note: Most of the debates begin with a brief introductory statement from each speaker that was shown as a tease early in the newscast. The debates begin with an introduction from moderator Howard K. Smith.

Howard K. Smith: . . . and two of the nation's most prominent and probably opposing commentators, Mr. William F. Buckley Jr.

William F. Buckley Jr.: My own notion, having got here just a little while ago, is that what the Miami Convention already proves is that the overwhelming amount of power happens to lie in the hands of conservative Republicans who are proving that the disaster of 1964 didn't have any strategic effect.

Howard K. Smith: And Gore Vidal.

Gore Vidal: To me the principal question is, can a political party based almost entirely upon human greed nominate anyone for president for whom a majority of the American people would vote?

Howard K. Smith: [For ABC News' convention coverage for this presidential election] two of our nation's most decided commentators have joined us this year. They are Gore Vidal, a former Democratic candidate for Congress, but better known as an author, of among many other things a play about a political convention, and William F. Buckley Jr., a former conservative candidate for the mayor of New York, but better known as a columnist, commentator, and editor of the *National Review*.

Mr. Buckley, who of the potential candidates do you think is, if I may steal a title from Mr. Vidal, the best man?

Buckley: Oh . . . I'm not prepared to say. I think that several of them are highly qualified to be a good president. I think what you really mean to ask me, but are too shy, is who do I like most? . . .

Howard K. Smith: (laughs)

Buckley: . . . to which my answer is that as a conservative I am very much fetched by the programs of Mr. [Ronald] Reagan and also of Mr. [Richard] Nixon. I think that Mr. Nixon has convinced the majority of the delegates that he is the best man in the light of his experience. Given also the fact that his experience coincides with his commitment to a series of policies which they endorse.

Howard K. Smith: Can Mr. Vidal assess those candidates for us? What do you think of?

Vidal: Well, I would come, I think, to a very different point of view. To me, none of them is really the best man, with the possible exception [of] Nelson Rockefeller. I cannot *possibly* imagine Richard Nixon as the President of the United States. I think he is essentially the "hollow man" that we always discussed. I think we're living in revolutionary times in which new programs are needed. And that you're going to need somebody who can rally the young people of the country. The Negroes, the ghetto, the poor are angry, restless. This is a terrible time, and here you have a man who when he was in Congress he voted against public housing, against slum clearance, against rent control, against farm housing, against extending the minimum wage. He was against . . . rather dubious about the 1954 Supreme Court decision bill. He said, "I am opposed to pensions in any form as it makes loafing more attractive than working." And now today he offers us a program for the ghettos, which he's made much of, and what is it? Well, he is going to give tax cuts to private businesses that go into the ghetto and to help the Negroes. Now, in actual fact, private business is set up to make private profits. There's nothing wrong with that, but it's not in the business of philanthropy. So they'll get their tax cut and we'll have nothing in the ghetto probably but the rising expectation of what is now revolution.

So I would say that as far as Mr. Nixon goes, I think he is an impossible choice domestically.

Buckley: Uh, may I comment Mr. Smith?

Howard K. Smith: Please do.

Buckley: Yeah, it seems to me that the earlier focus of (pregnant pause) Mr. Vidal here on human greed — you do remember? — he said that he found himself wondering whether a party that was devoted to the concept of human greed could ever hope to get a majority of the American people to vote for it. Now the author of *Myra Breckinridge* is well-acquainted with the imperatives of human greed.

Howard K. Smith: (laughs)

Vidal: I would like to say, Bill . . .

(crosstalk)

. . . If I may say Bill . . . before you go any further, I would like to say that if there were a contest for Mr. Myra Breckinridge, you would unquestionably win it. I based her entire style polemically upon you, passionate and irrelevant.

Buckley: That's too involuted for me to follow. One of these days perhaps you can explain it . . .

Vidal: You follow it.

Buckley: My point is that the number of people who are voting for the Republican Party agree that there are certain ways of doing things which are different from other ways of doing things. For Mr. Vidal to give us the pleasure of his infrequent company by coming back from Europe where he lives in order to disdain the American democratic process and to contemn a particular party as engaged in the pursuit of human greed requires us to understand his rather eccentric definitions. Is it greedy, really, for people to suggest that what matters to poor people is that they have houses? [It was] Senator Bobby Kennedy, not Mr. Nixon, who first suggested a tax rebate for businesses engaged in this kind of pursuit. Is it really greedy to want to preserve our freedom? Have the Republicans been greedy by being prepared to support a war which kills American youth and uses up 30, 40 billion dollars a year? It may have been wrong, but greedy would strike me as very wrong-headed.

Vidal: Well, by and large, however, it is a party which is based upon business interests. It represents only 27 percent of the people of the United States. Somebody once pointed out Republicans are not a party, they're a class. It is a class of, by and large, small businessmen with very strong views about not weakening the moral fiber of the poor who now number 30 million people. And by and large I quoted for you Mr. Nixon's record in the Senate, which was not terribly helpful as far as programs for the poor goes. They do believe, however, Republicans, in spreading the money around amongst themselves. They get, through big business, they get far more subsidies than the poor do. As a matter of fact we have a situation in the United States where they believe they should have socialism for the rich and free enterprise for the poor. The rich are subsidized and the poor, alas. I think our military budget is something like 75 billion dollars — and I agree entirely about the horrors of the war with Mr. Buckley — we are bound to agree on something — and only 2 billion dollars is spent for poverty programs, which all Republicans, to a man in the House and Senate, have been opposed to.

Buckley: The thing about the poverty programs and, of course, the thing about the democratic system is that there ought to be a party free to discuss that which is wrong in a particular concept. And it is widely acknowledged by a lot of people, many of them Democrats, that the poverty program hasn't worked. It's certainly acknowledged by poor people who are victims of the rather comfortable rhetoric of Mr. Vidal. The principal contributions that have been made for the elimination of poverty in America have been made by millions upon millions upon millions of people who have not sought political favor who work hard enough to create a surplus. Which surplus is distributed during the past four or five generations in this country resulting in the fact that we have the luxury of being able to focus on those who are poor in our midst as though we can do something about it, which is something that no other country less occupied with human greed has the luxury . . .

Vidal: The nice thing about the Republican Party is that every four years after denigrating the poor amongst themselves, referring to them as freeloaders, "They don't want to work," and I have many quotes here from Ronald Reagan and Richard Nixon on the subject, and making fun of the minority groups with lovely little remarks like, what was one of the headings in the *National Review* when Adam Clayton Powell got nabbed? The headline was "The Jig Is Up." Well, this sort of kind of pleasantry which you get in the Republican Party — I should say in the right-wing all over the United States. And then every four years you get this sort of crocodile tears for the poor people because they need their vote. Well, I don't think that they're going to vote for any of your candidates unless by some terrible accident the Democrats get split hopelessly at Chicago, which could well happen, and Eugene McCarthy's people do not vote. In which case I think Richard Nixon might very well become the next president and I shall make my occasional trips to Europe longer.

Buckley: Yes, I think a lot of people hope you will. (all laugh) As a matter of fact, Mr. Arthur Schlesinger Jr., who is a member of your party, not mine, reminds you of your promise to renounce your American citizenship unless you get a satisfactory party in November.

Vidal: Now, now, Bill, that isn't quite what I said. I said it would be the *morally* correct thing to do if the war did not end, but I can behave as immorally as the Republicans.

Buckley: I can believe that, too. Vidal makes the recurrent mistake of distorting my remarks in my presence — my remarks are not interesting to a national audience . . .

Vidal: That's true, Bill.

Buckley: Well, I'll try to interest them. When we discussed "The Jig Is Up" with Adam Clayton Powell Jr. the point precisely of that editorial was that Mr. Powell's invocation of the fact that he was a Negro in order to immunize him from many things — immunize him from committing libel, to immunize him from stealing the money that his wife didn't earn, to immunize him from the complete contempt of the proscribed procedures of the House of Representatives was not a satisfactory argument. That was grotesque. Now it is quite true that Reagan is capable of talking about freeloaders. So am I, because there *are* freeloaders. It is one thing to say that a society ought to concern itself with the plight of its poor. I think the Republican Party is saying that. But, it is quite wrong for any party to fall into such demagogic lengths as to suggest that everybody who is poor is poor simply because he cannot find work.

Vidal: However, that is the Republican line. Reagan, in cutting back the welfare with the Office of Economic Opportunity, he rejected something, very proudly, something like 12 programs. Now, these were programs not only to help the poor but to help them find jobs. Meanwhile, with several denunciations [by Reagan] which, if you like, I will quote you, on freeloaders on welfare and how it encourages immorality and divorce — I assume he was on unemployment insurance when he divorced Jane Wyman — and I suppose it is a wicked thing that people don't have money. But in actual fact, in California, those who are on those roles who can work but don't work they estimate to be about 5 percent. About 95 percent might have been helped by the Office of Economic Opportunity and he rejected [it] very proudly. He has the number one record of any governor in the United States for that. Though you did mention at the time in one of your columns that Pat Brown also rejected several of their programs. You were wrong. Pat Brown never rejected one.

Buckley: Your saying that I was wrong doesn't necessarily make it so. Mr. Vidal's problem is, I suppose, best exemplified by the fact that the American people in whose behalf he speaks with occasional eloquence seem to be able to get along very well without him. It was Mr. Reagan, notwithstanding the fact that like the Republican Party he ran on a platform advocating "human greed," won the democratic contest by a million votes, all of them Democratic votes since it was required to have a million votes. Now this being the case, it seems to me that they either are transcending your analysis or else they are so dumb that they don't benefit from your acuity.

Vidal: Bill, Bill, if I may say so, the electoral process often makes great errors. I think you would agree, according to you it's made nothing but errors since 1932 with a sort of eight-year interregnum of a man that you didn't much admire. In fact, you criticized Richard Nixon for his "unctuous love and attention" to the great general. I think unctuous is rather a good word here.

Buckley: I can account for these errors other than by using these neurotic terms that you are so fetched by. I say the Republican Party is here to do a responsible job. To suggest that they are here simply as an instrument of the exploitation of the people is to engage in a diseased kind of analysis which increasingly Mr. Vidal finds to his liking. Fortunately, it's not a national concern. Perhaps the Republican Party should have a platform in how to deal with Vidal. If absolutely necessary I will write it for them. But meanwhile . . .

Vidal: But meanwhile, I wonder what they are going to do with Reagan. I'd be very, very nervous. You have written lately of your intimacy with Reagan and with Nixon and that you've discussed the Vietnam War with them and that you are satisfied with their positions. Since you're in favor of the invasion of Cuba, since you're in favor of bombing the nuclear potentiality of China, since you're in favor of nuclear bombing of North Vietnam, I'd be very worried about your kind of odd neurosis — neurosis being a friend of anybody who might be a president. If I were one of the candidates I would say, "Bill Buckley, don't stay home."

Buckley: I would be very worried too, if you had such a *grand guignol* view — but I've never advocated the nuclear bombing of North Vietnam.

Vidal: You have. I'll give you the time and place if it amuses you.

Buckley: Well, you won't.

Vidal: I will.

Buckley: The nuclear bombing of Red China struck me as it struck John F. Kennedy as a viable proposal in mid-summer of 1963. I advocated the *liberation* of Cuba at the same time that Mr. Kennedy *ordered* the liberation of Cuba.

Vidal: No, no, Bill, don't step away from the record. You said we should enforce the Monroe Doctrine and invade Cuba, the sooner the better, in your little magazine whose name will not pass my lips [in] April 1965. You favored bombing Red China's nuclear production facilities the 17th of September 1965 in *Life* magazine . . . and you suggested the atom bombing of the North of Vietnam in your little magazine, which I do not read but I'm told about, the 23rd of February 1968. So you're *very* hawkish, and now if both Nixon and Reagan are listening to you, I'm very worried for the country.

Buckley: Now it seems to me that the Republican Party has shown a record of greater sobriety than Mr. Vidal, who boasts of not reading something which he is prepared to misquote in the presence of the person who edits it.

Vidal: Now, Bill Buckley, the quotation is exact . . . the quotation is exact.

Buckley: We know that your tendency is to be feline, Mr. Vidal.

Vidal: Yes.

Buckley: Just relax for a moment and think very simply on this: I have not advocated — I'm not horrified at the prospect . . .

Vidal: Bill, I just quoted whole sentences to you, when and where. Are you saying you didn't say it?

Buckley: I'm saying that I didn't say it, that your misquotations . . .

Vidal: Tune in this time tomorrow night and we will have further evidence of Bill Buckley's cold warrior turned hot . . .

Buckley: That's right, and about the human greed of everybody in the world except yourself. Tomorrow we'll have what Mr. Vidal thinks about the Kennedys.

Vidal: Goodnight, and let me tell you . . . (all laugh)

Howard K. Smith: Excuse me, gentlemen. It's been very enjoyable hearing you articulate two points of view that will be heard in two conventions in this month. Thank you very much indeed. I think I detected some unfinished lines of thought. We'll have time to follow them through tomorrow and tomorrow and tomorrow.

Debate Two — Republican Convention
Sunday, August 4, 1968
Miami Beach, Florida
(One day prior to convention)

Gore Vidal: Is the dovish plank on Vietnam a cunning device to get peace-minded voters to vote for war-minded candidates? I happen to be suspicious because in 1964 I voted for Lyndon Johnson — and peace.

William F. Buckley Jr: The platform is an excellent example of the capacity of a platform to reconcile different points of view. On the one hand, there is something in it for most Republicans. On the other hand, a dove-minded candidate could select and stress certain phrases, as could a war-minded candidate.

Howard K. Smith: The Republican platform completed earlier this morning and issued today says that the Johnson administration's Vietnam policy has failed in every respect and the Republicans now offer what is called a positive program for settlement based on self-determination, a course that will enable the South Vietnamese to assume increasing responsibility, but the Republicans will not agree to a peace at any price or camouflage surrender. Mr. Vidal, is that an adequate statement of what has to be done about Vietnam?

Vidal: Well, I think Mr. Buckley said it rather wisely at the top of the program that this was a plank on which both a dove and a hawk could run or take off from, to complete the metaphor. And I think the two principal candidates, of course Richard Nixon, obviously, and as an alternative I see Ronald Reagan. I would like to, as a public service, if I may, very briefly go through some of the positions that each of these men — just quotations that they have made — because I'm genuinely puzzled as to what they would do about the Vietnam War, and I think most people are puzzled and certainly the platform hasn't been much help. Ronald Reagan — I have five statements here that he has made in the last five years. The first is, "Peaceful coexistence is dangerous folly." That's the 7th of November 1963. Shortly thereafter on 15th of October 1965 he said, "We should declare war on Vietnam. We could pave the whole country and put parking strips on it and still be home by Christmas." A nice metaphor. Then in the 1st of April 1967 he favored, quote, "a step up of the war." Shortly thereafter, on the 24th of June of '67 he said, "We have the power to wind this war up fast. I think we should use it." Now this year, 25th of March, in *U.S. News and World Report*, Governor Reagan said, "Maybe the enemy ought to have some unrest in some corner of his realm to worry about," which sounds a bit like adventurism. He then said in the same article, quote, "This policy of accommodation asks us to accept the greatest possible immorality," so he's against coexistence with them. Then finally, just a few weeks ago, he said, "The war in Vietnam must be fought through to victory. We've been patient too long," and just a few days ago he said that Lyndon Johnson was trying to fight the war too cheaply. Now I'd like to ask Mr. Buckley, who is a friend of Ronald Reagan and has talked to him about the war. What will he do? Will he use ultimate weapons or will he accommodate with the enemy?

Buckley: Well, I think that Mr. Reagan has made it a lot more clear than, for instance, President Johnson has done concerning whom one could very easily produce a series of statements concerning the Vietnam War which are to say the least at least as confusing as these. I think Mr. Reagan has been pretty well clear that he is prepared to leave alone any country in the world which itself is prepared to leave *us* alone. I remember his enthusiasm for a formulation by Senator [J. William] Fulbright. Senator Fulbright said in 1967 in a highly quoted speech, "However the United States may despise as obnoxious the internal doctrines of any particular nation, we have no right to attempt to control or extirpate those doctrines unless there is an effort being made to export them." This precisely captures the spirit of Mr. Reagan's foreign policy and, for that matter, of my own. So that I think that what we have to worry about is whether or not during the past few years the great hallucinations under which we have been persuaded that there is in fact a politics of convergence. Whether those are dangerous hallucinations and this is really what the Republican Party, I think, is here to talk about.

Vidal: I think it's worse in, however, a candidate who as recently as two months ago was talking about the dangerous folly of peaceful coexistence. One thing we have to remember, that there are more communists than there are us. We are a minority in the world, and I would think that a militant hawk who would like to embark us on other foreign adventures like Vietnam would be a very dangerous person to have. And apparently Mr. Richard Nixon is in agreement. An obscure statement of his which is extraordinarily dovish, and to my mind very sensible, in October of '67 in *Foreign Affairs* he said [he seriously questions] whether the American public or American congress would now support a unilateral American intervention even at the request of a host government. So apparently I would say that Nixon was going to have an extremely difficult time [with his Republicans] leading him into foreign adventures in Vietnam . . .

Buckley: I don't think any Republican — at least none that I can think of — this is a problem that Mr. Vidal will face more intimately in Chicago — I don't think any Republican is daunt- ed by the mere fact of numbers. There are far more communists in the world than there are Democrats, far more than there are Americans, so far as we can tell. Of course, the communists don't go in for free elections so it's difficult to stipulate the pop- ularity of their regimes. Our force in the world is based on the leverage which is one part moral and one part technological . . .

Vidal: If I may make a point there. We have absolutely no moral right to be in Vietnam. I'm afraid we haven't got time to go into that in great detail. We have absolutely forgot all morality when we did not live by the Geneva Accords . . .

Howard K. Smith: We have about 30 seconds. Can Mr. Buckley have those 30 seconds for a rebuttal?

Buckley: There is a lot of cynicism in any platform. For instance, there is one phrase that says, "Nor have we forgotten the Cuban people who still cruelly suffer under communist tyranny." What that really means is, "Nor have we forgotten to forget the Cuban people who still suffer under communist tyranny." This is, after all, a political convention, not a convention among tablet keepers. Under the circumstances I think they are doing pretty well.

Howard K. Smith: Thank you very much Mr. Vidal, Mr. Buckley. I'm sorry we don't have more time, but we do have four more nights and we'll make the most of them beginning tomorrow.

Debate Three — Republican Convention
Monday, August 5, 1968
Miami Beach, Florida
(First day of convention)

William F. Buckley Jr.: It seems to me, to judge from the rhetoric of the Republican Party here at Miami Beach so far, that it shows the signs of strain from years of a general assault on American values which in recent days has come to a high pitch in the caterwaulings of professional critics and even expatriates. The GOP says it ought to win next November, as indeed I think it should, but it hasn't found out how to say why.

Gore Vidal: Tonight the key question for every patriot is can an aging Hollywood juvenile actor with a right-wing script defeat Richard Nixon, a professional politician, who currently represents no discernible interest except his own.

Howard K. Smith: On the floor at this first day of the Republican Convention we've heard a few all-right speeches and quite a few ho-hum type speeches. We would like now to demonstrate how the English language ought to be used by two craftsmen, our guest commentators: William F. Buckley Jr., a conservative Republican, columnist, and commentator and one-time candidate for mayor of New York, and Gore Vidal, author of among other works John Kennedy's favorite Broadway play, a play about a convention called *The Best Man.* Mr. Buckley, you've studied the potential candidates, which two do you think would make the strongest Republican ticket?

Buckley: I should think that among those who are nowadays being considered, the two strongest would be Mr. Nixon and Mr. Reagan. I say that not only because I consider them to be competent, but because I do feel that both Mr. Nixon and Mr. Reagan have a sense of communicable conviction that the Republican Party has something distinctive to offer. [There is] a little bit too much in some of the others of the sense that schematically the Republican Party ought to arrive at position A-B-C this particular year. But the other two, I think, grew up in the Republican Party with some sense of mission.

Howard K. Smith: Mr. Vidal, can you make the onerous effort of hypothesizing yourself a Republican for just a moment and say which two you think would be strongest if you wanted a win for the Republicans?

Vidal: Well, that's quite easy for me since I don't think of myself as a Democrat either. I would say that watching the convention this morning it became quite clear to me that John Wayne and his daughter would be the ideal ticket for the party (laughter). But thinking about the country's interest, I would say that if Rockefeller and [Charles] Percy were a ticket they could certainly do very, very well in picking up a great deal of disaffected Democratic votes, particularly if McCarthy should be spurned in Chicago, which may very well happen. I could see about half of the young activists in the McCarthy movement coming out for Rockefeller and Percy. Rockefeller and Reagan would certainly be a much more certain ticket for the Republicans to win with. But if they did win, I wouldn't like to be Mr. Rockefeller. Somebody from Orange County might speed up the electoral process. All in all, I would say that Rockefeller was the best man for the independents and Democrats that might vote for Republicans.

Howard K. Smith: One of the conspicuous features of this convention has been the way all the Republican leaders have played down ideology. There have been no floor fights; none are scheduled. The platform wasn't really fought over. This is good perhaps for winning votes, but it does blur the rationale of the Republican Party. Mr. Buckley, what does the Republican Party stand for now? Is it in flux or what?

Buckley: Yes, it is in flux. Actually, all political parties should be, to a certain extent, in flux. The question is whether or not the Republican Party believes strongly enough in a series of convictions to convince a lot of voters that there is inherent in the Republican view of life a certain stability which is associated with the growth of the United States. If I may say so, Mr. Smith, it's extremely interesting and extremely lively to sit by and watch professional critics of the Republican Party burlesque people whom the Republicans themselves tend to like. You may have forgotten that a few moments ago we were treated to Mr. Gore Vidal, the playwright (Vidal smiles and nods in mock courtesy), saying that after all Ronald Reagan was nothing more than a quote, "aging Hollywood juvenile actor." Now, to begin with, everybody is aging . . . (Howard K. Smith laughs)

(crosstalk)

Vidal: Even you are, Bill. Perceptibly, before our eyes.

Buckley: Therefore, that adjective didn't contribute anything extraordinary to the human understanding. Then he said, "Hollywood." Now one either acted in Hollywood during the time Mr. Reagan acted or one didn't act at all. Mr. Vidal sends all of his books to Hollywood, many of which are rejected, but some of which are ground out and put on.

Vidal: Now Bill, I don't send any there.

Buckley: He called him a juvenile actor, which is presumably to be distinguished from an adult actor. My point is . . .

Vidal: Yes, get to it.

Buckley: If you play this sort of a game you can say, "Look, I don't think it's right to present Mr. Gore Vidal as a political commentator of any consequence since he is nothing more than a literary producer of perverted Hollywood-minded prose."

(crosstalk)

Vidal: Now, now Bill . . . careful now.

Buckley: I'm almost through . . .

Vidal: In every sense.

Howard K. Smith: Let Mr. Buckley finish this sentence then, Mr. Vidal, I assure you time to refute.

Buckley: [If] ABC has the authority to invite the author of *Myra Breckinridge* to comment on Republican politics, I think that the people of California have the right when they speak overwhelmingly to project somebody into national politics even if he did commit the sin of having acted in movies that were not written by Mr. Vidal.

Howard K. Smith: How about Mr. Vidal's answer to that now?

Vidal: Well, as usual, Mr. Buckley, with his enormous and thrilling charm, manages to get away from the issue towards comedy. He is always to the right, I think, and almost always in the wrong. And you certainly must, Bill, maintain your reputation as being the Marie Antoinette of the right-wing, (Buckley makes a pretense of not listening) continually imposing your own rather bloodthirsty neuroses on political campaigns. In the case of Ronald Reagan, I say he is a juvenile actor in the sense that that was pretty much what he was cast as. As a presidential candidate, which is, after all, what we are talking about . . . [here is] a man who as of yesterday was saying that the administration is trying to pour down our throats what might have been good medicine during the days of the Depression, but he said, "The patient got well a long time ago." That means the United States. This will come as news to the 30 million poor people, it will come as news to people in the ghettos, people that, I'm afraid, voted against you so heavily when you ran for mayor, Bill, when you kept reminding the Negroes in Harlem that, what is it?, their landlords came up tippy-toe, in one of your favorite verbs, and threw the garbage out of the windows for them.

Buckley: You are pretty hard up . . .

Vidal: A man who has finally said, as of yesterday morning, Ronald Reagan says, "The only function of government is to get out of our way and leave us alone as much as possible." Now on this occasion I'm afraid I have to agree with William Buckley, the distinguished thinker, when he says — my favorite quotation from you; I have a treasury here — "Today as never before the state is a necessary instrument of our proximate deliverance." As usual, in your slightly Latinate and inaccurate style, but you do feel, as most of us do, that the state must have some responsibility for what happens in the country. And now you have a Ronald Reagan, whom you approve of, who does not want to use the Federal government to do anything at all.

Buckley: Mr. Smith, I confess that anything complicated confuses Mr. Vidal. This has been plain for a very long time. He has a great difficulty reconciling even axiomatic positions concerning political philosophy. But I was invited here and I am prepared to try to talk about the Republican Convention . . .

Howard K. Smith: Yes.

Buckley: . . . but I maintain that it's very difficult to do so when you have somebody like this saying that Mr. Nixon, who is about to be nominated, I gather, from listening to you, that he is running for no, quote, "discernible purpose other than his own best interest." Now what does that mean, "discernible"?

Vidal: Would you like me to tell you what it means?

Buckley: No, not until I'm through examining.

Vidal: Ah, yes. Sorry.

Buckley: He has won every single primary contest that he entered. He has shown to be a heavy favorite in every poll conducted among Republican voters and independent voters.

I have no doubt that he would lose some democratic elections if the vote were limited to WASPish Democrats who like to live out their life in Rome. Why does he say "no discernible political interest," except, presumably, because he likes to be naughty, which has proved to be a professionally highly merchandisable vice.

Vidal: Not unlike your so public vices . . . (unintelligible) wickedness, Bill. You say that for "no discernible reason" is he running. Well, I'll tell you why I'm dissatisfied with him and I think most of the country should be somewhat alarmed. He has no position on Vietnam at all. This is a major issue in the United States. It is a major moral issue. It is a major economic issue. What does Nixon say on this? Well, he wants to have a summit with the Russians. (Vidal impersonates Nixon's voice) "A hard-hitting summit meeting," he says. This is, incidentally, the candidate the Russians most detest. This may be very helpful the fact they hate him to a few [George] Wallace-ites, but it is not going to do him much good at a conference. He issued an economic statement. What did he come out for? Higher interest rates. And then for the ghettos what does he have to say about what is in effect a civil war in the United States? Well, he'll give tax deductions to businesses that want to go and work in the ghetto. He'll install a computer to tell him where the jobs are. I don't call that much that's discernible to the naked eye except somebody playing it very safe to get elected.

Buckley: Mr. Vidal, your description of the naked eye hardly fits that of somebody who is moderately well-informed. I have no doubt that there is somebody in Haight-Ashbury or Greenwich Village who considers that your caricature is fetching, although I don't. Mr. Nixon has elaborated at some length his position on Vietnam. He is committed to the rightness of that endeavor in Vietnam. He does believe that the United States government, as a result of a schizophrenia which is bound in, Lyndon Johnson has not vigorously prosecuted what is in fact a war, a war which he relates to our own best interests. For you to suggest in the process of attempting to accelerate Democratic achievement that all he has done is speak in such burps is hardly to do him or you a service.

Vidal: (with mocking niceness) I'm so happy to see your elegant prose style at its very best tonight, Bill. It's very inspiring to those of us listening to it.

Buckley: I think you're being sarcastic.

Vidal: But I wonder, really, if Nixon is going to prosecute this war. Seriously, one would like to know what he's going to do. He's ruled out atomic weapons already. He's pretty much ruled out an invasion of the North. He does want, in some way, to cool it, but he won't tell us. Now I think he ought to. I would also be interested to know would he be interested in your project, since you are a great friend of his and professional entertainer of the far right. Does he favor your plan for bombing China? The nuclear capacity of the Chinese? In a very moving piece called "A Blow for Peace" in that magazine I will not mention on the 29th of December 1964 . . .

Buckley: We know that you'd like nothing to sully your lips.

Vidal: You will eat it first. You came out in favor of "history aches for such an act of greatness." That is the bombing of the Chinese nuclear capacity. In 1965 you came out with the same [statement].

Buckley: Do you want to talk about my background? I'd be delighted to.

(crosstalk)

Howard K. Smith: Some administration Democrats have said they could accept that Vietnam plank in the Republican platform.

Buckley: (straining to hear Smith's question) They could accept which plank?

Howard K. Smith: The Vietnam plank in the Republican platform.

Buckley: Yes, it is an ambiguous plank. And there is no question but that the war in Vietnam having been so badly fought, not as the result of any failure in our military but as a result of a failure in our policy, has led to a great confusion. The war in Vietnam is not justifiable in the opinion of Mr. Nixon unless it in fact represents a salient, which is armed by the communist world, however loosely spoken of, which is directed against our best interests. It was because Mr. Kennedy and subsequently Mr. Johnson believed that it was, in which point of view every single one of the people who are professionally charged with evaluating America's interests concurred that it was that we went to war there. But we failed to win it. The failure to win it has caused a number of developments not least of which is the domestic turmoil from which Mr. Vidal and his party seek to profiteer.

Howard K. Smith: Mr. Vidal, what would you consider a satisfactory plank, briefly and generally, on Vietnam?

Vidal: Well, you're not going to get a satisfactory plank, certainly not out of the Republican Party. One did not get it, nor will you, probably, out of the Democrats. Everybody is slightly afraid of the dove/hawk labels, and I think the platform of the Republicans is one, as I keep pointing out, anybody can run on it, a hawk or a dove. I think a satisfactory one would be an admission that the American empire has certain very plain limits. That it was an immoral act going in there to begin with by not holding the elections which the Geneva Accords of 1954 guaranteed. We then came a cropper. We have everybody to thank for it; we have [Dwight D.] Eisenhower to begin with, mildly, Kennedy a bit more so, and Johnson, the super hawk. I'm not at all convinced that Barry Goldwater, had he been elected president, wouldn't have been just as much of an activist. But these empires are very dangerous things to possess . . .

Buckley: [Goldwater] would have won the war.

Vidal: . . . as Pericles once pointed out. Once you get one it's very difficult to let it go. But if we don't let it go it's going to wreck us economically. We're already in trouble. It has certainly divided the country at a time when resources should go to the slums and to the poor and for trying to revive an extremely shabby country.

Buckley: The country is not quite so shabby as Mr. Vidal believes.

Vidal: It will be shabbier after the Republicans get in.

Buckley: The figure "30 million poor" is, of course, a figure completely at the mercy of largely arbitrary statistics as to what constitutes poverty. Let me just put it this way — that if the same figures nowadays used in constant dollars to produce 30 million American poor people had been used in 1929 then 65 percent of the American people would have been judged poor by those standards. The point is, of course, the Republican Party is aware that there is not nowadays an American imperialist movement. No doubt there are those who believe that we want to be in Vietnam because the Chase National Bank struggles to establish a branch there. This is the hobgoblinization of the Marxists . . .

Howard K. Smith: Gentlemen, you have just about one concluding sentence apiece. Can you give us one? Mr. Vidal?

Vidal: I would say that Mr. Buckley, as always, has misstated the case on poverty as he has on much else. There are over 30 million people living at the poverty line, and the Republican Party according to its platform, which I have read very carefully, is going to benefit the insurance agencies, the private interests in great detail, and nothing at all of the people.

Howard K. Smith: Mr. Buckley?

Buckley: I think that it is something for which all of us have to be grateful that there are left in America people who believe in the democratic process sufficiently to know that occasionally people can penetrate such myths as have been energetically projected by Mr. Vidal and that they choose not to avail themselves of the alternative that Mr. Vidal offers them up, which would be not only a philosophy and an economy of stagnation, but also a spiritual world of stagnation.

Howard K. Smith: Thank you very much indeed, gentlemen.

Debate Four — Republican Convention
Tuesday, August 6, 1968
Miami Beach, Florida
(Second day of convention)

Howard K. Smith: One of our guest commentators, William Buckley, was out in Miami today making a speech to an organization called The Young Americans for Freedom. Buckley said in his speech that an ad in this morning's *Miami Herald* listed as "paid for by Citizens of Black America for Rockefeller" was almost certainly paid for by Rockefeller himself in a last ditch bid for delegates. So at an afternoon news conference this question from a foreign reporter:

(ABC News switches to a video segment)

Foreign reporter directing question to Nelson Rockefeller:
As a journalist I appreciate Mr. Buckley very much. But I think this allegation, you should comment about it. Did you personally pay for [the advertisement] or didn't you?

Nelson Rockefeller: I didn't. But I think we ought to

recognize that Mr. Buckley did have an unfortunate fall on his boat (crowd of reporters laughs heartily).

(ABC returns to studio set)

Howard K. Smith: Mr. Buckley, does that impregnate you with a wish to comment?

William F. Buckley Jr.: I wouldn't have put it quite that way (all laugh). I think there are two interesting questions involved, none of them having anything to do with me. The first is, was the ad objectionable? If it wasn't objectionable then we're all wasting our time. I find it extremely objectionable because here's an ad that says that no Negro American will vote for Mr. Nixon or Mr. Reagan if he is nominated by the Republican Party. It is signed by 30 or 40 Negroes led by Mr. Louie Lomax. Now why won't they? Because they said they want to be able to choose between candidates who are quote, "pledged to racial justice." Elementary logic therefore leads us to conclude that Richard Nixon and Ronald Reagan are *not* pledged to racial justice. This is in my judgment a slur if it's not true. Now, there's no documentation in this ad at all. The question arises, who floated the ad? My judgment is that we are not here in Miami in order to be naïve. With the kind of philanthropic excesses with which Mr. Rockefeller has floated money around the country in order to further his cause, I ask you to judge, or the viewer to judge, who most likely paid for an ad described merely as, quote, "paid for by Citizens of Black America," — a non-existing organization up until the time of this ad — "Louie Lomax, Beverly Hills, California, Chairman."

Howard K. Smith: I'm going to assume that Mr. Vidal doesn't want to defend any Republican candidate on that score, but I will ask him a question. Ralph Abernathy came here today and one of his leaders said that he thought the Republican Party was trying to win this election with a backlash vote and without Negroes. Do you think that's a fair comment?

Gore Vidal: I think it's a fair comment. I don't think it's of any great moment who paid for the ad. I do think it's a very good point in the ad that the Republican Party — [at] this convention here only 2 percent of the delegates are Negro. I think right off that gives you an idea that in a sense this is what they call a lily-white convention. The two front runners which I happen to regard — unfortunately Rockefeller is not one of them, even though he seems to be doing my dialogue for me tonight. Nixon and Reagan as the front runners I would say would be completely objectionable to most of the Negro citizens of the country particularly in the cities, which is where the swing vote is. It's the cities that decide elections. Nixon lost in 1960 largely because of the Negro vote which shifted in the industrial states in the main cities.

There is no reason on the platform or anything else why he should do any better now. His record is very, very bad. On the 1954 Supreme Court decision on integrating schools he said in 1959, as Vice President he said, "The administration's position has not been is not now and should not be immediate integration." Now this is an extraordinary thing for an executive officer to say four years after a Supreme Court decision. Recently, he said, notice, on the subject of urban crime, he said, "It is better to double the conviction rate than quadruple the funds for poverty."

Of course, he wants law and order on the street, which is the magic phrase this year, but he does not necessarily want justice and order. One interesting thing on this law and order thing: between 1900 and 1960 there were 50 race riots in the United States, all of them begun by white people. At the end of these riots nobody asked suddenly for crime bills. Now all of a sudden the Negroes are beginning, for what I happen to think are, by and large, rather good reasons, to bestir themselves to try and get action. I think that response is pretty plain. And then finally Mr. Nixon said, "I'm very proud to say," this was just recently, "I've been in politics for 22 years (imitates Nixon's voice) and have never had a racist in my organization and don't have any now." He neglected to say that his Southern campaign manager is Howard "Bo" Calloway who is a militant segregationist from Georgia. So I don't think that Mr. Nixon is exactly the ideal candidate to get any votes from the black population.

Howard K. Smith: Mr. Buckley, do you think the Republican Party is trying to win a backlash vote?

Buckley: Well, it takes always a certain amount of time to unscramble Mr. Vidal's statements, but let me make a heroic effort in one or two sentences. Point one, Mr. Nixon was backing civil rights bills way before John Kennedy was in point of historical circumstance. Point two, the time to back a civil rights bill, you may have noticed, is as of the moment when it becomes popular. Up until that moment it becomes completely forgivable if you don't do so. Lyndon Johnson is considered a great friend of the Negro people, but he voted against a whole series of civil rights bills over a period of years. Point three, some 30 to 35 percent of the Negro people voted for Nixon in 1960. I think somebody ought to get around to telling us what it is that Mr. Nixon has done since 1960. that alienates those votes. No, here's what's happening. What's happening is that the Democrats are trying very hard to mobilize all of the Negro votes on a racist basis. On the one hand, they tell us we shouldn't treat people as simply members of a race, members of a group. On the other hand, they're always trying to deploy them as members of a group, members of a race. What Mr. Lomax and whoever paid for this ad, and I'm sure it was the Rockefellers right out in Los Angeles, are doing is to encourage the notion of stereotypes. If you don't like Nixon's views on atomic energy, then he doesn't believe in racial equality. This is an old technique, but I think that some of us ought to agree that it's sordid, even left Democrats.

Howard K. Smith: Mr. Vidal?

Vidal: I'm sorry, Bill, I wasn't listening. (all laugh)

Buckley: You haven't been listening for years. (all laugh)

Vidal: I know, I haven't been hearing much here. No, I was thinking ahead to the issues while you dealt with the personalities. I was thinking how Ronald Reagan, he's the other front runner. He's had a very mysterious career. He was a left Democrat, as you so happily put it. In 1950 he campaigned for Helen Gahagan Douglas, known as the Pink Lady by Richard Nixon, her opponent. Incidentally, when I remark about him as an aging juvenile, I should say he is an aging juvenile actor, but I admired him very much as an actor. He was extremely good in *The Voice of the Turtle* and particularly in a movie called *A Hasty Heart*, which was the only occasion he had ever been outside the United States. They made that on location in England. He took a turn to the right, however, when he married the daughter of a very conservative brain surgeon — where is the rest of him? — and he went to the right-wing. In 1962 he campaigned for John Rousselot who was one of the officers of the John Birch Society. In 1964 he campaigned for Charlton Lyons who was a segregationist governor, a would-be candidate for governor of Louisiana. He also campaigned for a character called Lloyd Wright who was a senatorial campaigner . . .

Buckley: Hey, how long does this go on, out of curiosity?

Vidal: You are curious . . .

Buckley: You've got more time than I have?

Vidal: I think it goes on just to get the record. What I'm trying to spell out here is any man who supports Birch Society candidates as of '62, a segregationist candidate as of '64, is not exactly a friend of the Negro. Finally, he is against all welfare out in California. He takes great pride in having cut all the Office of Economic Opportunity programs. He cut as many of those programs — which are to get jobs for Negroes — as many as Pat Brown.

Howard K. Smith: I think Mr. Buckley is going to sue us for equal time in a moment. We'd better let him talk.

Buckley: Mr. Smith, I assure you there that is as great a congestion of factual errors in what Mr. Vidal just said as can be found anywhere in the world. Number one, Nixon never referred to Helen Gahagan Douglas as a Pink Lady. Number two, Ronald Reagan never campaigned for her. Number three, he did not turn to the Republican Party until seven years after he married his present wife. Number four, when he backed John Rousselot, it was not known that he was a member of the John Birch Society. How am I doing? Okay?

Vidal: Not very well.

Buckley: . . . of the fact, which interests me very much, because if I were Mr. Vidal, I would pride myself that I could smear Ronald Reagan by actually saying things about what he has actually done. It strikes me as extremely revealing that so frenzied is he for ammunition against him that he is simply going back and melodramatizing his past, and simply concocting a polemically useful past career for him. But this is fiction.

Vidal: No, it's very nicely put. You haven't made any points that I can see. He was still campaigning for various segregationists. He obviously knew whether they were. Whether he knew Mr. Rousselot was a member of the Birch Society, I don't know . . .

Buckley: You realize that those segregationists that you mention are members of the Democratic Party? How do you allow anybody to be a member of the same party whose representatives down South are militant segregationists without saying, "I, Gore Vidal, swear that I shall never again touch pitch in the Democratic Party"?

Vidal: I would say . . .

Buckley: You're talking about Democrats, not Republicans.

(crosstalk)

Vidal: Mr. Lloyd Wright is a Republican running against Kinkel [**Editor's Note:** No reference found for this person.] in the primary. No, the point is that he has played along with that racist line in general . . . he has referred to unemployment insurance as a "prepaid vacation plan for freeloaders" . . .

Buckley: There is no segregationism in the Democratic Party?

Have we terminated that point?

Vidal: No, we haven't. I think we are making some points that he isn't going to get many Negro votes. On the other hand I don't think he's going to be nominated either, so it's probably academic.

Buckley: Is it right that nobody should vote for a party whose Southern representatives are racist?

Vidal: Oh my dear Bill, you must not get into the subject of the sins of the Democratic Party because I will not defend the Democratic Party. Wait 'til Chicago for that.

Buckley: Well, you have been for years. You ran as a Democrat. How dare you?

Vidal: Indeed, I did.

Buckley: How dare you run as a Democrat?

Vidal: And you ran as a Conservative and now you are pretending to be a Republican.

Buckley: I ran as a Conservative . . . there are no racist Conservatives in New York City.

Vidal: There are *no* racist Conservatives in New York City?

Buckley: Certainly not, certainly not, not that I've located.

Vidal: Hmmmm . . .

Howard K. Smith: Mr. Buckley, what about the question I asked? Do you think the Republicans should seek a backlash vote?

Buckley: Mr. Smith, I hope I'm too old to reply to your question in the terms in which you put it. A backlash vote is something which by definition you don't seek out, right? So therefore one shouldn't seek out a backlash vote.

Howard K. Smith: If you stimulate it.

Buckley: If you say ought there to be a backlash against the kind of sly racism suggested in this pro-Rockefeller ad I say yes there ought to be. Now if you want to call it backlash, okay, but make certain what it is that we are talking about. I think that we should oppose racist stereotypes of any sort. That it is wrong to say all Negroes will vote only for the guy who agrees with them on every single policy . . .

Howard K. Smith: We have less than one minute left. Can Mr. Vidal answer, then you may make a final statement?

Vidal: If I may add to that . . . I liked that eloquent gesture forward. I'll remember that. What matters is not who paid for the ad, but that there were several hundred, I gather, names there — I looked at it just before the program — of American Negroes, many of them quite distinguished. So I, therefore, if they feel this way you can hardly attack them for racism since they are the patent victims of racism.

Buckley: So educate them so they don't feel that way . . .

Vidal: Would you like to educate Martin Luther King? . . .

(crosstalk, slightly heated)

Howard K. Smith: I think the Republican, Mr. Buckley, should have that last 15 seconds.

Buckley: I simply say when people sign something obviously benighted like this accusing Mr. Nixon of not desiring racial equality decent people who are bipartisanly concerned for the future of this country ought to say, "Don't pull this off, don't try to get away with it."

Howard K. Smith: Thank you very much indeed, Mr. Buckley, Mr. Vidal.

Debate Five (Part One) —
Republican Convention
Wednesday, August 7, 1968
Miami Beach, Florida
(Third day of convention)

Editor's Note: Curiously, Buckley and Vidal debated twice on August 7, the third day of the convention. Apparently one debate was aired live for the eastern United States and the second debate, also live, for the western states. Moderator Howard K. Smith has virtually the same opening remarks and begins the debates with the same question directed toward Vidal. As the debates unspool, however, the remarks from one debate to the other are very different.

Howard K. Smith: . . . the subject for William Buckley and Gore Vidal on *Second Look* tonight, beyond the nomination.

Gore Vidal: In the last few days, Richard Nixon, the Lazarus of American politics, has set the tone of his campaign: nostalgia. Once nominated he will go to Russia, as General Eisenhower went to Korea, and once the election is over, he will serve all the people in the great tradition of Thomas E. Dewey.

William F. Buckley Jr.: It looks like Nixon, nobody is really surprised, and no committed Republican feels cheated. What was the fuss all about?

Howard K. Smith: While we're waiting for the demonstrations and the rituals to come to an end we would like to call on our guest "controversialists." That's the term the BBC in London invented and it's good. I beg our guests to look beyond the nomination and suggest to us when the convention is over and the campaign actually begins, what issues can the Republicans use profitably to win? For example, today the polls said that Vietnam is still far and away America's biggest worry. Now, if Mr. Nixon wins — he has been about as hawkish as President Johnson — can the GOP use that issue effectively?

Let me introduce our guests: Mr. William Buckley, editor of the *National Review,* who ran for mayor of New York and said that if he won his first act would be to demand a recount. And Gore Vidal, author, who ran as Democrat for Congress and says he got more votes in his district than any Democrat since 1910 — but he lost. First, Mr. Vidal.

Vidal: Well, I've been following the convention with great care and the platform and the positions of the various candidates. And you ask, really — Can this party win? What issues [will they] take to the country? It's hard to tell. There are three important issues in the country. One is Vietnam, the other is the race war, third is poverty. Assuming that Mr. Nixon is the candidate, which I suspect he will be, he has moved from the position of hawk to what seems to be dovish. On the race war he has contributed very little and neither has he on poverty. Whether he can excite the country, I haven't a clue. He is very adept at being sort of all things to all men, and I've noticed that this afternoon there was a story which the Nixon people have denied, but it was rather interesting, rather typical. There was a taping during a Southern caucus which they didn't know about and Mr. Nixon said privately, "I personally am against open housing, but I have said that I'm in favor of it just to avoid a fight here at the convention." Well, this is normal political procedure. We won't go into the virtues or demerits of open housing. The point is that this excessive adaptability that he has is not exactly inspiring. And yet to be fair, at the same time it is, after all, compromise is one of the conditions of democratic politics.

Howard K. Smith: Mr. Buckley?

Buckley: Well, I think that Mr. Nixon has endeavored to compromise, but I think at the same time he has endeavored to lead, no doubt in the wrong direction Mr. Vidal and others believe. But still it seems to me that he has attempted, cogently in my judgment, to mobilize the Republican Party into a party of responsible opposition. Now as regards to Vietnam, I think that Mr. Nixon is enough a member of the contemporary scene to recognize that an enormous paralysis has set in on the basis of which it becomes impossible to prosecute that war as it might have been prosecuted, say, beginning in 1965, back before President Johnson found himself in that schizophrenic paralysis which had made it impossible for him either to pull out or to prosecute the war vigorously. As regards the issue of race, I think that Mr. Nixon has for years stirred with those Republicans who believe that there is a role for the federal government to play in urging racial reconciliations, but that he has always believed, as I think all Republicans and an increasing number of Democrats believe, the federal government can't A., do it all, or B., even do that much of it which is necessary to genuinely satisfy and bring about a total racial harmony.

Vidal: I think that the federal government can, of course, not do it all. Nobody can do it all. I think both left and right in America and center are both — are all concerned about this bureaucracy that we hear a lot about at this convention. But at the same time, when you make a program — I have had the fortune or misfortune to have read all of Richard Nixon's position papers in this campaign and to listen to him say, "Well, we must get private enterprise into the ghettos and when you do that, this will somehow solve it and we'll give them a tax credit or a tax deduction for doing that." Well, I can just see that business is out to make money. It is not philanthropic. Once they take the tax cut I think that's the last we'll see of them. Now you began, Mr. Smith, began by asking how Richard Nixon, if he's the candidate, and we assume he will be in a very few minutes, that if he goes to the nation at a point in history when you have the young people absolutely disaffected, not only in the Democratic Party but practically the two-party system over Vietnam, and all he tells us — he has not confided anything to us except that he's going to have a tough summit with the Russians who don't much like him. Well, I don't know how that is going to turn out. That's not exactly a program. We have a race war going on in the cities. He comes up with practically nothing except there is to be a computer so the people can press the button, you know, and get your ideal job. This isn't enough because we've come to a moment in history where we really have, we are on the verge of a revolution. It doesn't take any prophet or even anybody slightly alarmist to see what is happening in the cities of this country at this very moment. And to have a man of the old politics come out with the old smoothing (imitates Richard Nixon's voice), "Well, we are all working together in this thing," representing largely business; I think that if Richard Nixon were elected for President it would be an absolute — no matter with what good will — it would be a disaster because the young, the black, the poor are disaffected and I don't see him ever drawing them to him.

Buckley: Well, I think that Mr. Vidal has a point. Probably not the one he sought to make, which is that a lot of people who are poor and disaffected, especially when you think of, for instance, students of Columbia University or Berkeley University are precisely happy in being disaffected and it's going to be very, very difficult for anybody to persuade them that they might just as well cease being alienated and try just for a change developing some sort of enthusiasm for their own country. I do think this, that it is impossible for anybody in the middle of a war running for President for three, four, five months before the election to elaborate an exact policy of disengagement. Adlai Stevenson was in my judgment wrongly taunted in 1952 precisely for his failure to elaborate a specific way to end the Korean War. What we have to do is study what Mr. Nixon has said and extract from it a series of dominant attitudes on the basis of which we can assume what is the likely intelligible role that he will play. Concerning this business of worrying that he is devising means by which people can, quote, "make money," in the course of building buildings or destroying ghettos or whatever, I don't think this really ought to be a matter of concern. It seems to be that Mr. Vidal, if he pauses to meditate on the fact, will recognize that most of the publishers, for instance, who have brought out the major works of literature throughout the history of the civilized world did so intending to turn a profit. And I don't think really that we should worry about the 2, 3, 4, 5 percent that is made in profit by people who labor in tearing down a ghetto and building a desirable substitute.

Howard K. Smith: What can we judge Mr. Nixon by? Now, we've not seen him in an executive position. We have seen Governor Rockefeller for quite a while in an executive position. We've seen . . .

Buckley: What would you call the Vice President?

Vidal: Hardly executive.

Buckley: Oh, legislative?

Vidal: Well, he is the presiding officer of the Senate. That is a legislative situation.

Buckley: National Security Council.

Vidal: As we remember General Eisenhower couldn't really remember what he had done, which is rather in the eight years what made the issue . . .

Buckley: Now Mr. Vidal, why do you want to vulgarize something like that? In the first place, he didn't say that.

Vidal: Frankly, what he did . . .

Buckley: You want to remember what he said? Because I remember.

Vidal: He did say — indeed he said, "If you gave me a week I might think of something."

Buckley: No.

Vidal: Or perhaps that's a little too succinct for Eisenhower.

Buckley: That's right, yeah, yeah.

Vidal: That's the general idea.

Buckley: And it's not succinct enough for you.

Vidal: More than enough, what he precisely is . . .

Buckley: Mr. Eisenhower was asked to ascribe to Mr. Nixon the authorship of a single important project that came into law and he said . . .

Vidal: No.

Buckley: "If you give me a while, I'll think of it."

Vidal: No, it was more succinct than that. In any case, why . . .

Buckley: My point is . . .

Vidal: Why do you want to vulgarize it by going into such detail?

Buckley: Because my point is that Mr. Eisenhower has taken every opportunity he has been able to find in the past seven or eight years to pay tribute to the executive capacities of Mr. Nixon, which as a matter of fact nobody doubts. I mean, who doubts his executive capacity?

Vidal: Well, I doubt it right here.

Buckley: If you do, then you're very hungry for really viable sources of discontentment over Mr. Nixon.

Vidal: Oh, good heaven . . .

Buckley: But he's the kind of person who would get General Motors or any of those things to run at a million dollars a year.

Vidal: Are you sure of that?

Buckley: Of course I'm sure of it. He's a man of manifest competence. Criticize him because you don't like his ideas or because of what he has alleged to have said to somebody about open housing.

Vidal: I don't think that will do, but I must say I agree with Eugene McCarthy who said that "Administrators are a dime a dozen and it's very easy to hire one." So in that case, perhaps it isn't all that important, but it was interesting how you changed the bidding of the last set of statements. By talking about when I was talking about the people in the ghettos and the poor of the country, the disaffected, you talk about Columbia and Berkeley, which is a very exciting subject to Republicans. They don't like them. They have beards and immoral manners. But what I was talking about was the 30 million people in the country who are living at the poverty level. What is to be done about them? What are you going to do about war budgets, a whole country that is geared to war?

Buckley: Well, yeah, well.

Vidal: We have a 75 billion military budget. We have 2 billion dollars for poverty, and Mr. Nixon tells us it is a "cruel delusion," unquote, he says, "to tell the Negroes that they can expect anything at all out of the budget this year." We must have less expensive . . .

Buckley: Mr. Nixon knows something that you don't, Mr. Vidal, which is that this country has had the most phenomenal success of any country in the world in graduating people from poverty into affluence, and that graduation has been the result of economic and private activity, not government activity. And under the circumstances he wants to maintain . . .

Vidal: That was another era.

Buckley: . . . those wellsprings of action.

Vidal: I'm afraid that has changed.

Buckley: Oh no, the media, no, it's only changed . . .

Vidal: It's now static. Poverty is static unfortunately.

Buckley: It's only changed if you succeed in changing it. If you get us nice and socialized like India then we'll all be poor. You can continue to live in Rome.

Vidal: Does it appeal to you, however, and you may be joining me there faster than anybody else, that in the United States 5 percent of the population have 20 percent of the income and the bottom 20 percent have 5 percent of the income?

Buckley: I think this is irrelevant.

Vidal: This seems to me . . . I know that you revel in a kind of inequality.

Buckley: No, I think it's sort of because . . .

Vidal: Because then this is based upon that.

Buckley: You see, I believe that freedom breeds inequality and that's . . .

Vidal: Say that again?

Buckley: Freedom breeds inequality. Now I'll say it a third time.

Vidal: No, twice is enough. I think you made your point, yes.

Buckley: Unless you have freedom to be unequal there is no such thing as freedom. Every single person who owns a Ford car today is considered, by terms of international statistics, as being especially privileged. My point is that he worked to achieve it and that we ought to encourage a system which permits people like you and people like Mr. Smith and people like the technicians in this room to make progress. The fact that they make more progress than other people is not their fault nor is it the fault of other people. It's the fault of freedom, but this I judge to be a price that we ought to be willing to pay in order to indulge the great animating force of progress in the world.

Vidal: Don't agree . . .

Howard K. Smith: Mr. Buckley, what do you think is the strongest line or the strongest attitude that Nixon could take in the campaign that follows if he gets the nomination?

Buckley: I think the strongest line that he could take is to face the people of the United States and say, "The reason, the principal reason, for the discontent of our time is because you have been encouraged by a demagogy of the left to believe that the federal government is going to take care of your life for you." The answer is the federal government A. can't, B. shouldn't, C. won't. Under the circumstances look primarily to your own resources — spiritual, economic, and philosoph-ical — and don't look to the government to do it because the government is going to fail you.

Vidal: Well (sighs), what can I say?

Buckley: Not much.

Vidal: You have given that ghastly position once again.

Buckley: Yeah.

Vidal: Of the well-to-do and those who inherit money and believe that others do not . . .

Buckley: This is such balderdash.

Vidal: . . . but somehow achieve equality, but if, you know, sort of like the Goldwater caper.

Buckley: Yeah.

Vidal: But in actual fact you are going to have a revolution if you don't give the people the things they want. Now I'm putting it to your own self-interest, they are going to come and take it away from you. Now I'm sure you don't want them to take the *National Review* away from you and run it in Watts . . .

Buckley: And inherit my deficit?

Vidal: (laughs)

Buckley: Listen my friend, Mr. Vidal, if you really believe that the way to address the people of the United States is to say to them, "Unless we give you precisely what you want, you are entitled to come and take it, to burn down the buildings, to loot the stores, to disrespect the law." Then I say that you do not recognize that you are an agent for the end of democratic government. Because the people of the United States . . .

Vidal: It seems to me, if I may say something, let me give you just a little thought for the day. "It seems to me narrow and pedantic to apply the ordinary ideas of criminal justice to the straight public contest." Who said that?

Buckley: Oh come on, Mr. Vidal, look.

Vidal: It is one of your favorite figures said that.

Buckley: Yeah. I don't know whether you are even aware . . .

Vidal: You don't recognize it.

Buckley: . . . that the majority of the people who were arrested in Washington D.C. for looting in the April riots were earning in excess of $125 a week. It was a caper as far as they were concerned.

Vidal: You think, ah, it was a caper.

Buckley: It had nothing — yeah, they were employed, well employed.

Vidal: Wouldn't you say that when people were well-employed and they were rioting there was something wrong with the society?

Buckley: They are alienated. They are alienated. And they are alienated for the same reason that people like you are alienated.

Vidal: Ah, you are alienated.

(crosstalk)

Howard K. Smith: We are running low on time.

Vidal: You are the minority position in politics in the country.

Buckley: I believe in America.

Howard K. Smith: We are running low on time.

Vidal: Which America?

Howard K. Smith: Can we stop on the words "Which America?"

Vidal: "Which America," very good.

Howard K. Smith: Thank you, gentlemen. I hadn't designed that by the way (laughter).

Debate Five (Part Two) —
Republican Convention
Wednesday, August 7, 1968
Miami Beach, Florida
(Third day of convention)

Howard K. Smith: While we're waiting for the ritual to end
and the balloting to begin, I'd like to call on our guest "controversialists." That's a word invented by the BBC in London and
a very good one. I beg them to look beyond the nomination
and to suggest when this convention is over and the campaign
begins, what issues can the Republicans use effectively to win?
For example, I'm thinking of the polls today which showed
that Vietnam is still far and away America's biggest worry. If
Mr. Nixon wins the nomination, is he not about as hawkish
as President Johnson? Can the Republicans use that issue
effectively? Let me introduce the guests: Mr. William Buckley,
the editor of the *National Review* who ran for mayor of New
York and said that if he won, his first official act would be to
demand a recount; and Gore Vidal, the author who ran as a
Democrat for Congress and got more votes in his district than
any Democrat has got since 1910, but lost. First, Mr. Vidal.

Gore Vidal: Well, it's difficult. I think any political campaign depends pretty much upon who is the candidate. I think it's pretty plain tonight, unless there's some extraordinary surprise out here on the floor, that it's going to be Richard Nixon. And frankly, I'm sort of puzzled by the man. I mean, he's going to have to do something on the peace issue. I think he has moved his own position from extreme hawk to, I would say, rather moderate. He's made many sort of loose remarks today, talking about whether he's going to meet with the Russians and we're going to sit down and have a conference. Very unlike the old Nixon.

I think one of the things about his character, he once said something very interesting. He said, you know, the best example of a combination of idealist and practical politician is Theodore Roosevelt. When he wanted to get something done, he would compromise all over the place, and I suspect that really is the kind of candidate [Nixon] will be. He will adjust himself to the issue and who knows? He might even be, heaven help us, a good president, though I certainly doubt it.

Howard K. Smith: Mr. Buckley?

William F. Buckley Jr.: Well, I think that Mr. Nixon recognizes that the Vietnam situation is in flux. The reason why it is in flux it seems to me is suggested by Mr. Nixon's analysis during the past couple of years. Namely this, that the President of the United States has not, as a result of a division within his own party, succeeded in coming out with a truly intelligible explanation of what it is that we're doing there and what it is that we ought to do in order to get out of there. Under the circumstances, I myself predict that the Vietnam issue is not going to be a great issue during the campaign. That it will largely be a period comparable to that during the summer of 1952, the Korean period, during which discernible differences between Mr. Eisenhower and Mr. Stevenson weren't really what mobilized the electorate. Rather a feeling that one person as distinguished from the other would be able to approach the problem with a fresh perspective and a sense of national energy which the incumbent couldn't dispose of.

Howard K. Smith: What other issues are there? What issue do you think can be used effectively?

Buckley: Well, I think two, primarily. Number one, law and order. I wish there was a way of saying law and order that didn't make critics say, "Oh, you're talking about the racial question now." I would like to know how to say law and order by other means, but still mean law and order. It is a deeply significant issue and one of the problems that we face and that Nixon's got to face is this: what do we do about the growth of really mutinous members of the American community? People who say look, "I don't care about what the community says. I don't care what the majority says. As far as I'm concerned, I'm going to follow my exquisite conscience and do precisely what I desire to do."

These people have got to be faced not only politically but philosophically, and this is something which in my judgment Mr. Nixon has got to elevate into the status of a genuine national debate.

Howard K. Smith: Mr. Vidal, what's your comment on that?

Vidal: Well, I think this, of course, is an area in which Nixon's own conscience may be indeed exquisite. I don't think he himself is going to be much use. There's an interesting story in the papers tonight. Somebody went into a Southern caucus with a tape recorder, unbeknownst to the caucus and unbeknownst to Nixon, and Nixon said to the Southern caucus, "Of course I am against open housing and I want you to know this. It was a bad decision, I know, but I had to come out for it openly. Otherwise there would be a fight at the convention, but I want you to understand that." Well now, open housing — first of all, this is again Richard Nixon adjusting to the political realities, and perhaps it would be cruel to say he shouldn't do it. After all, he is a politician.

But I don't think that he has any plan at all other than just trying to keep it as cool as possible because he doesn't come from a party which has, as far as I can think of, any ideas at all. His own plans for ghettos are, I think, one computer to tell people where to find jobs. As for the mutiny in the land Mr. Buckley refers to, of course there's mutiny in the land. When you have 16 million people in poverty and 16 million people in abject poverty, and these are actual statistics, and when something like only 10 to 11 billion dollars is needed to end it all, according to health education welfare, I suspect that you're going to need some sort of a program, and this year, this convention has been fascinating to me because not only has there been no ideology or what there is is subliminal and done in code, but there have been basically no programs at all, so I'd be, I'm just, I must say about Mr. Nixon's campaign, I'm just curious. I don't know what he'll do.

Buckley: Well, in, in the first place assuming that Mr. Vidal can create a statistic by simply promulgating them, the answer is that there isn't such a correlation as he suggests. If there are 16 million people today below the poverty level, so were there four years ago, and so were there eight years ago, and so were there during all of those years when we have had a beneficent Democratic administration. The point of the fact is that most of the people who are leading the way to mutiny are *not* the poor. They are the William Sloane Coffins and the Dr. Benjamin Spocks and it's these people that I think we need to concern ourselves about if we are concerned for the future of the democratic experiment. Now, I have no doubt that an effort is going to be made, as Mr. Vidal just finished making it, to assume that there is a dark, anti-Negro prejudice implicit in Republicanism. It is an effort that has already been successfully made. Let me give you a very brief example.

Last night, Mr. Vidal said only 2 percent of the people who are here in Miami Beach as delegates are Negroes. This is a considerable affront considering that they represent 11 percent of the American population. I did a little probing into the statistics and I find out that the percentage of Negroes who registered with Mr. Gallup, their preference for the Republican Party is 2.4 percent, so that they are, roughly speaking, adequately represented here on a one man, one vote basis. Whereas the Democratic Party, you have 15 percent of the people who are registered as Democrats are representing the

Negro population and yet they have only a 5 percent representation. Now, just as I think it's wrong for a Republican to say that the Democrats are by these tokens anti-Negro, so I think it's wrong for Democrats to reason oppositely from undernourished statistics.

Vidal: The statistics are well-nourished Bill, and the two percent reflects the fact that the Negroes feel there's nothing much to be gotten for them in the Republican Party, nor is there. Well, and incidentally, while we're on statistics, to finish once and for all, Ronald Reagan. I did some checking last night when you contradicted me that whether Mr. Reagan campaigned for Helen Gahagan Douglas. Indeed he did. He made several radio speeches. You said that . . .

Buckley: (Talking over Vidal) Indeed, he did not.

Vidal: Indeed he did, and also, when he campaigned for Rousselot the only issue in that campaign, who was a Republican, was that he had been a member of the John Birch Society, and the other two, contrary to what you said, were not Democratic candidates that he had campaigned for, they were Republican — just to get the record straight.

Buckley: You have not, excuse me, you have not illuminated the record. You have confounded it.

Vidal: I have absolutely not. You must not react to facts so emotionally.

Buckley: (Talking over Vidal) I always react to facts.

Vidal: These are facts, however . . .

Buckley: It seems to me that Mr. Reagan's position on the John Birch Society is crystalline, has always been clear. He has always deplored it. The sharpest critic of Mr. Reagan in Sacramento is the single member of the John Birch Society . . .

Vidal: (Talking over Buckley) Yes, I read that.

Buckley: . . . Senator Schmidt. Yes, you read that, but you wouldn't have brought it up, but let's not go into that digression . . .

Vidal: (Talking over Buckley) He did, however, support a Birch Society candidate and he knew he was one.

Buckley: Let's simply ask this, well, why . . .

(talking over each other)

Howard K. Smith: It sounds as though Mr. Nixon is going to be, maybe, the candidate, and Reagan is unlikely . . .

Vidal: I know, but I like Ronald Reagan. I like talking about Ronald Reagan (laughter). I mean, after all. We'll be nothing but Nixon from now on.

Buckley: Now, what I was trying to say is very simply this, that it is unfortunately a part of the polemical resources of both parties to try to insinuate that the other party is unfeeling concerning something. My point is that the Republican Party has only had 7 percent of the Negro vote because the Democrats have succeeded in persuading the overwhelming majority of the Negroes that the Democratic Party shows them an avenue to real progress. But we've had Democratic administrations not only in the states but federally, and the failure of them, in fact, to chart a course of true progress may, in fact, for the first time have the effect of reawakening an interest in the majority of the Negro community to alternative ways of progress. Those are extra-political ways, the kind that Mr. Reagan is engaging in in California.

Vidal: Very good, Bill, very good. I just sort of feel a . . . I feel a waffling now. I have a sense out there there's a convention going on, and, hmm . . .

Buckley: Does that mean you don't know what to say?

Vidal: No, I know what to say. I just finished saying it — that Richard Nixon has come out against open housing and he has explained to the Southern caucus that he said one thing to the public and another thing to . . .

Buckley: Lots of people come out against open housing — the Democratic mayor of Milwaukee — have all fought against open housing for years because it's wrong. It's unconstitutional.

Vidal: Yes, yes, and my Aunt Fenita's against it, too, but we're talking about Richard Nixon who's running for president.

Buckley: I know, but you only bring it up because . . .

Vidal: Because he's running for president. We're talking about Richard Nixon.

Buckley: No, because you assume that one can draw certain inferences from it. Are you trying to suggest that Mr. Nixon is delinquent in a morally sensitive area?

Vidal: I would say that Mr. Nixon was, has proven himself to be, all things to all men, if I may quote Saint Paul to you, and he continues to do so, and I am disturbed . . .

Buckley: Why does he lose elections? If he proved that, why did he lose an election if he proved that he was all things to all men? Come on. Why? Why? Why?

Vidal: Because . . .

Buckley: Because?

Vidal: Because it doesn't always work and you can't fool all people all the time, except perhaps on television.

Buckley: (Talking over Vidal) Then he didn't prove . . .

Vidal: I think you're sweating. Here, take this (Vidal offers tissue to Buckley).

Howard K. Smith: We have a report that Nixon has denied that he made that statement about open housing. I give it to you for what it's worth.

Buckley: Yeah, I'm sure he didn't make it. I'm sure he didn't make it.

Vidal: And I'm sure he did make it, so . . .

Buckley: No, I'm sure he didn't make it at all, but I think one has to remember that it is one thing to simply formulate a position which is pleasing to any minority group, whether it's Catholics, about prayer in the schools, or Jews about Israel, and Negroes about whatever, and simply to promulgators, (unintelligible) Civil Rights Bill of 1968, and then proceed to accuse everybody who voted against it as being anti-Semitic, anti-Negro, anti-Catholic.

Vidal: I must say . . .

Buckley: It's an old labor device and fortunately not totally successful.

Vidal: I must say that this is one of the strangest countries on earth that nobody's record ever matters at all. I must say that I think the public's memory is about four weeks, at best, and I say this sadly on all issues. I've tried . . .

Howard K. Smith: I'm afraid I'll have to interrupt you, but I ask you to meditate on the best choice for a vice president tomorrow because that's what we're going to be talking about. I thank you now and we'll be back with more on Miami day three, the nomination.

Debate Six — Republican Convention
Thursday, August 8, 1968
Miami Beach, Florida
(Fourth and final day of convention)

William F. Buckley Jr.: There's a sense in which the Nixon/ Agnew ticket is saying to America, "Look, this is the way politics in this country, Republican and Democrat, have worked for a great many years. We think that American politics have worked successfully and therefore we've got to try more of the same."

Gore Vidal: As of yesterday, Nixon's the one and now tonight [Spiro] Agnew's the other one. The Grand Old Party has done it again.

Howard K. Smith: So four days of unity proved too much of a strain for the Republican Party and at last it produced a rebellion, a futile rebellion, but one happened on the floor, and now it's been stifled. Agnew has at this point more than 800 delegate votes, far more than enough for nomination. He and Nixon are now in the hall. Our two guests, Gore

Vidal and William Buckley, are here.

I would like to ask our two commentators if they feel that Agnew's presence on the ticket might have sacrificed victory for unity. Mr. Buckley, you're the Republican. You go first.

Buckley: I think that the selection of Mr. Agnew is consistent with the imperatives of democratic politics, of American politics if you like. The idea is a generally balanced ticket. It interests me that so many charges have been raised since the nomination of Mr. Agnew to the effect of, is this being done to appease the South? Nobody seems to ask whether or not the mere suggestion of Mr. [John] Lindsay was, quote, in order to appease the North. The answer is, of course, in both cases, the answer would have been yes, the Republican Party is guilty. It does want to appeal to the South. There are *people* in the South.

It has become very fashionable to suppose that people in the South don't count and shouldn't count, but they are voters. They have a political point of view and Mr. . . . the choice of Mr. Agnew, is in my judgment a sophisticated choice. It seeks to do two things simultaneously. One, to nominate somebody whose position on civil rights is impossible to challenge. He was enthusiastically endorsed by *The Washington Post* and *The Baltimore Sun*. Two, somebody who since his election has insisted that civil rights is not a mandate for civil disorder.

Howard K. Smith: Mr. Vidal, what do you think about Agnew on the ticket?

Vidal: Well, Agnew is certainly a good governor and a generally responsible if nationally dim figure as of this date. I disagree with Mr. Buckley. I think that obviously a deal was made, perhaps back in the days when Agnew was supporting Rockefeller and suddenly switched over. This might have been the price of it. I think also when Reagan was beginning to cut into the Southern delegates Senator [Strom] Thurmond and the power group in the South simply said, "You're going to have to, Mr. Nixon, go along with us on proposing a candidate for vice president who will not be objectionable to us." I think of the lot, Agnew was probably the least disturbing compromise, but if you're looking at it to win an election, the votes are still going to be in the cities.

Lindsay isn't just the North, Lindsay is cities, Lindsay is somewhat the new politics, Lindsay appeals to youth. I would think Nixon would have been wiser either to go with Lindsay or if he wanted to play it the other way, to go the other extreme, go with Reagan, who, after all, can cut deeply into the [George] Wallace vote.

Howard K. Smith: What about that, Mr. Buckley? Do you think it would have been wise to choose one side or another rather than reach a compromise on a candidate who is not well-known?

Buckley: Well, conceivably so, but you have to bear in mind that Reagan excluded himself. If Mr. Reagan had said this morning, "I'm willing to go," I think it altogether likely that Mr. Nixon would have chosen him because he is extremely well-known and he is an extremely persuasive candidate. But he ruled himself out. Therefore, having done so, who are we then left with? I think that although Mr. Agnew is inconspicuous nationally, this is a campaign that is going to be dominated by Mr. Nixon and incidentally, I think that this very likely figured because had he chosen a Lindsay or a Rockefeller or somebody like that who always sort of proceeds as though he was front and center himself, it might have been difficult to organize the kind of harmony which I think somebody running for the presidency of the United States is entitled to. You don't want a prima donna running alongside you if the ultimate responsibility is yours.

Vidal: I think that is probably true enough. I was very struck — perhaps Mr. Nixon will tell us about it later — I was very struck after he was nominated last night, this is a moment that should be of inspiration to the country. It's rather a great thing to be nominated for president. Nixon did something I've never seen a presidential new nominee do. He talked about the technique of how he got the nomination, about how after Oregon he thought it was set, and it was quite candid. It was very beguiling in a way that he talked about the technique of being nominated, and I kept waiting for an "all right now, you are the nominee of a major party. Say something to us." You know, inspire us. I mean, you know, without being unduly corny about it, this is a troubling time and I was fascinated by Nixon, the technician, at such a grave moment, and I wonder really how he's worked it out and at what point will he begin to say, now, this is what I'm going to bring to the country on Vietnam, etc.

Buckley: Well, I think that this is naïve and that Mr. Vidal, as a novelist, ought to recognize that when artists relax, they tend to talk the least about their achievements. If you talk to Maria Callas after she has made an enormous impression at the Metropolitan Opera singing a title role, she isn't likely to say to you, "Do you want to know how I practiced to hit that high E?" She is likely on the other hand to speak about, oh, her costume or her rehearsal or something.

Vidal: (Talking over Buckley) Yes, but still . . .

Buckley: I think it altogether natural that Mr. Nixon should not have gone into the substance of the Republican philosophy at that moment.

Vidal: Right, but if I may continue your image, on the day that Maria Callas gets married I don't think she would talk about her high E. I think indeed she would talk about what the marriage meant to her and might get on another subject.

Buckley: Well, I think it's a matter of taste and I think that anybody . . . The difficulty with politics is, of course, that people tend to be pompous and if you had approached Mr. Nixon last night at three o'clock in the morning and said, "Mr. Nixon, tell us about the extent to which Edmund Burke has influenced you," he would have looked pained and for the best of reasons. At moments like that he'd much prefer to speak about Checkers [Nixon's dog] or the Oregon delegation or what novels he had recently read.

Vidal: (Talking over Buckley) I think all of this is true (unintelligible).

Buckley: (Talking over Vidal) . . . understandable and desirable.

Howard K. Smith: Something terrible has happened. I think you both agree that Agnew is a pretty good candidate, a pretty good governor.

(talking over each other)

Buckley: Well, I, I . . . Excuse me.

Vidal: Go ahead.

Buckley: Here's what I think is exciting about Agnew, and my knowledge of him is as limited as that of the majority of the American people. I think that he is onto something, a devotion to civil rights plus a devotion to the notion that civil rights doesn't mean that you have to be tolerant towards people like Rap Brown and Stokely Carmichael and the 228 sit-ins that he arrested last spring and this incandescent show of law and order. When you get a fusion of those two attitudes, you might find the Republican Party contributing something to the common will, which it very sorely needs.

Howard K. Smith: Is that your view of Mr. Agnew, Governor Agnew, Mr. Vidal?

Vidal: It's not my view, but I reserve judgment on him. I think it's an unwise choice. In other words, I think Nixon and Agnew are going to lose the election and that makes me perfectly happy, but I'm trying to look at it from what their point of view is, and he is certainly a perfectly decent man to run and lose. What is fascinating about Nixon on the one hand, I must say, we accuse him of being an opportunist and he certainly is, but occasionally he is unduly principled and this is perhaps principled in the wrong way and it may well be, I think, tonight has in a sense contrived his defeat. But we'll know more about that in November.

Buckley: Well, we do know, I think, that it is the way of people who seek the presidency or reelection of president to promise the vice president to everybody. When Franklin Delano Roosevelt used to do it, everybody thought it was sort of cute, you know, and the liberal intellectuals would say, did you get that? He promised to Jimmy Burns and Harry Truman and Henry Wallace simultaneously — get that, old pro. But when it's done by a Republican we get all solemn and censorious, you know, and now it's sort of evil.

The point is that American politics operate in a certain way. There are sanctions and there are punishments. One of the sanctions is the deployment of the vice presidency. I think that if Mr. Nixon had nominated somebody who was demonstrably irresponsible then we could all get into a sweat over it, but he hasn't done it and even Mr. Vidal is a little bit unconvincing in his opposition.

Vidal: Well, I would only say that I also have an interest. My brother-in-law is the insurance commissioner of Maryland. I think I would bring this up, Bill, before you bring it up. So I'm playing a familial game on this. I would say in general, however, that what we have seen practiced here the last few days is very profoundly to my mind the politics of irrelevance, that the issues of the country have not been dramatized. They have hardly been discussed. It has all been technicians' work, balancing out, which is the democratic process. We'll see it again in Chicago, Bill.

Buckley: No, Mr. Vidal, you are completely wrong because you understand, you don't understand, in America the great issues are never discussed in a convention. They're always discussed *before* a convention. A convention is simply that crystallizing process on the basis of which positions which have been arrived at before go through certain mechanical processes on the basis of which certain verdicts are delivered, but for you to suppose that Chicago or Miami Beach is the place where people accost themselves with great opposing metaphysical verities is to suggest another society than our own. It's never happened in America. Never ever ever ever.

Vidal: Oh yes. There have been great issues, certainly, before great conventions. I attended in 1940 the one in which Wendell Wilkie was nominated.

Buckley: (Talking over Vidal) What were the issues? What were the issues? Absolutely nothing.

Vidal: Quite fascinating. They kept shifting, but in any case . . .

Buckley: (Talking over Vidal) The issue was who'd be nominated.

Vidal: What you're up to in a case when we're in the midst of a war which not much of anybody likes, where do we stand? And if anybody votes for Nixon, they honestly don't know what he's going to do and I say this having been stunned in '64, like 24, or what was it, 28 million Americans who voted for Lyndon Johnson? He was voted for because we thought that he was a peace candidate against what looked like a potential war candidate. And what happened? Johnson did not confide in us, as it turned out, and became an extremely aggressive war candidate and we all regret having voted for him.

Buckley: Well, not all, but the majority of the Democrats polled last week are in favor of Lyndon Johnson's performance of his presidency.

Vidal: (Talking over Buckley) As a matter of fact, it wasn't (inaudible) 38 percent.

Buckley: (Talking over Vidal) Don't, don't, don't . . . There's an unfortunate tendency to confuse yourself with the majority of the American people. Unfortunate from both points of view.

Vidal: Well, you speaking as a minority in which in our ecumenical grasp we shall never have. That is quite another thing.

On the other hand, I think that there is going, there's a quiet majority in the country which we're going to hear from. If for only saying no.

Buckley: Well, it may very well be . . .

Vidal: (unintelligible) process . . .

Buckley: It may very well be, but I do think that Mr. Nixon has, and in this sense he is both applauded and criticized, he has made his position on Vietnam about as clear as a human being's can be without saying if you vote for me I'm going to send the 17th Regiment to make a bridge attack around the 17th parallel. That's not the way that presidential politics . . .

Howard K. Smith: Let me ask you again about Mr. Agnew. Mr. Nixon won most of the states and far most of the counties in 1960. He won the South as well, yet he lost the election because he lost the cities. Is there possibly a stronger vice presidential candidate who could win the cities for him better than the one he's chosen? Possibly Governor [George] Romney?

Buckley: You've got George Wallace, Mr. Smith. This session in Miami Beach would undoubtedly have proceeded differently but for the brooding on the presence of George Wallace, and George Wallace is very likely going to cost the Republican Party the election of the presidency. Under the circumstances, it becomes a matter of urgent common sense for the Republican Party to attempt to present somebody who is not racist, who has a clear anti-racist record who nevertheless can appeal to the South and offer a program to the South which will undercut Mr. Wallace.

Vidal: In which case, if I may just make a very direct question to you, why not take Reagan who could really cut into — without going into too much Mr. Reagan's private . . .

Buckley: I told you. Mr. Reagan said he wouldn't take it. He wouldn't run.

Vidal: Yes, I remember, but if anybody's chosen by a convention, they tend to take things — they can be talked into it.

Howard K. Smith: May I tell you the news that the party is reunited again? The first roll call, Romney got 132 votes, and Agnew 1,128. Then it was made unanimous by voice vote after Romney himself moved it be made unanimous. So, Agnew is obviously the running mate. Would you please continue? I'm sorry to have interrupted you. But . . .

Vidal: No, we like listening to you, Howard. Say something more. Something ecumenical to suit our mood tonight.

Howard K. Smith: Well, Mr. Buckley, you talked to the Young Americans for Freedom the other day. Now they tell me that very soon half the American people will be under 25 years of age. There's now a constitutional amendment being prepared to give more and more of them the vote. Take the vote age down to 18. Is the Republican Party in a position to appeal to them? Are they going Democratic?

Buckley: I don't know that the Republican Party has taken an official position. I hope that if it does, it will take a position against extending the franchise. I think a much better case is made for limiting the franchise. There is no reason at all to suppose that people acquire political wisdom at about the same time that they walk into biological pubescence. The two are unrelated.

Howard K. Smith: Judging from the mail I've had this week, some don't acquire wisdom even after a very late age indeed.

Buckley: Yeah, well, of course. The answer is that the tendency of a democratic society is always to extend the franchise because if you're caught suggesting it, the assumption is that the people whom you finish enfranchising are going to vote for you for having suggested it.

Vidal: I think that's much too cynical. I'm for extending the franchise, though I must say I would share with Mr. Buckley a kind of, not a sense of confidence in the general majority . . .

Howard K. Smith: By my notes, Mr. Buckley's had the last word on the past two nights and we now have about 45 seconds left. Let's let Mr. Vidal have the last word.

Vidal: Well, I just say how much I've enjoyed these little chats that we've had, Mr. Buckley and I, and I think that if we've been a bit on the dull side we must remember that in the land of the free to be serious is to be solemn, but I in any case particularly admire his new book, *Myra Breckinridge* (laughter).

Buckley: It will be serialized in *National Review.*

Vidal: Yes.

Howard K. Smith: Thank you very much indeed, and I hope you won't go away because there have been complaints that issues have not been stated, and we have two brilliant acceptance speeches coming up which no doubt will say a great deal about issues and I hope you'll be available to comment about those. In any case, you will certainly be back, I'm delighted to know.

The Democratic National Convention, 1968
Chicago, Illinois

Debate Seven — Democratic Convention
Saturday, August 24, 1968
Chicago, Illinois
(Two days prior to convention)

Gore Vidal: Is it possible for a political party deeply split between hawks and doves, racists and integrationists, rich and poor, [to] nominate the best man?

William F. Buckley Jr.: The tragedy of Czechoslovakia points up the dilemma of the Democratic Party, the party that preaches peace and leaves the world periodically in shambles. Lyndon Johnson's uncertain war in Vietnam has proved as disastrous as his politics of unrealism in Europe. And now the Democrats are here to choose between a man who desires to exaggerate the worst of Johnson's policies in Vietnam and another candidate pledged to perpetuate the worst of Johnson's policies in Europe. No wonder the convention is a shambles.

Howard K. Smith: Our guest commentators, William Buckley and Gore Vidal, are with us in Chicago after their successful debut as convention commentators in Miami Beach. William

Buckley, conservative commentator, columnist, and editor of the *National Review*, on the defensive in Miami, may now take the offensive. But I beg to put the first question to Gore Vidal, author, playwright, increasingly also a commentator. Mr. Vidal, do you feel more comfortable philosophically here than you did in Miami?

Vidal: Philosophically? I wonder if that word will ever be used again while we're here in Chicago? I feel more at home in a way. Miami Beach was a sandbar with a drawbridge and a rather homogenized convention. This place is, as Mr. Buckley proposes, a shambles, it's a police state. One's aware of the horrors of the world here, the smell of old blood, the shrieking of the pigs as they are slaughtered in the morning. All this reminds one of life and death. And I think the conversations that are going on now about Vietnam to me seem to be particularly urgent and philosophically two sides are being pretty well-represented. In a sense I do feel at home in a way, but not happy.

Howard K. Smith: Mr. Buckley, what do you think will be the main weaknesses the Democrats will display here in convention assembled?

Buckley: I think that the principal weakness of the party at this point is the collision between its ideology and the practical consequences of its ideology. In other words, if they had been able to show to America that in return for having elected a Democratic president four years ago and a Democratic Senate and a Democratic House something was done to greatly speed America along its way to help America achieve stability and a sense of security, then there would have been a different attitude here among the Democrats. Primarily, I think what's bugging them is that they don't really know what to do and under the circumstances are clutching, as so many people do under the circumstances, at ideological straws.

Howard K. Smith: You mentioned the Czech crisis a while ago. What effect do you think the Czech crisis is going to have on the two parties?

Buckley: It ought, I should think, to have at least this effect: to convince us that the romantic politics of convergence, the politics that presuppose that the Cold War, as Senator McCarthy put it last April, is, quote, "over," are, as I say, politics of romance. The real world isn't behaving according to that particular paradigm, and that under the circumstances the leadership which presupposed the separatism of the satellite states is a leadership that made certain false assumptions of critical strategic consideration. I should think that those who view the disaster in Czechoslovakia wonder whether or not the Democratic Party has in fact achieved a foreign policy which has aided the humanitarian impulses of the liberalizing forces behind the Iron Curtain.

Howard K. Smith: Mr. Vidal?

Vidal: Well, in actual fact, there is nothing that the Democratic

Party can do about the Czechoslovakian affair any more than there's anything the Republican Party can do about it. Great empires behave badly. I think you could equate, if you wanted to, the Soviet intrusion into the affairs of Czechoslovakia with our own caper in the Dominican Republic when we moved in there against a government, a possible government, of which we felt we might disapprove and wanted so close to home. Empires behave this way, they behave very badly. I don't think anybody's happy about what's happening in Czechoslovakia, but the Democrats can do no more about this than the Republicans could do anything about Hungary despite John Foster Dulles's great talks about opening wide his arms for all defectors from the East. The one good aspect of the Czechoslovakian thing has been in the last five days the defection of the French and the Communist parties from Moscow. I suspect this in the long run is a good deal more important than the sad affairs of one country.

Buckley: It seems to me that the attempt to equate what we did in the Dominican Republic and what the Soviet Union has just finished doing to Czechoslovakia is at least depraved. It takes not into consideration at all the entire history of America's interventions in foreign countries during the past 20, 25 years. We have occupied, mostly on liberating missions, 18 to 20 countries, each one of which we have subsequently withdrawn from. In many cases we have withdrawn from countries that have asked us to annex them. On the contrary, the Soviet Union has never tolerated an election in Czechoslovakia, which we instantly set up in the Dominican Republic.

Nevermind the uneasy and self-serving attempts to excuse ourselves by pointing out the Dominican Republic. The fact is that the Democratic Party in 1964 issued a campaign platform a phrase in which committed the Democratic Party to quote, "encourage by all peaceful means the growing independence of the captive peoples living under communism" and citing Czechoslovakia exactly. What have we in fact done to encourage them? Another platform plank says, "We pledge unflagging devotion to our commitments to freedom from Berlin to South Vietnam." It certainly isn't unflagging, is it? And, finally, they say that they want us to do everything to, quote, "speed the restoration of freedom and responsibility in Cuba." If in fact America can't devise a foreign policy that seeks to effect those goals, why do they bother to create the rhetoric and why don't people like Mr. Vidal criticize it at the time?

Vidal: I think that's an awfully good question. Why do we continually, in both parties, maintain an impossible rhetoric which we cannot live up to? We have not the means, we have not the power, we have not the will to free Eastern Europe from the Soviets any more than the Soviets, hopefully, [have] the will to free certain of our client states from us. I'm happy to see you doing your homework, Bill, that you quote from the platform of the Democrats. I have lost my John Foster Dulles file, but it is absolutely a reflection of all the things that Dulles was saying since 1954 about containment, and all that is, I think — I quite agree — it is totally irrelevant rhetoric and I wish we'd stop it.

Buckley: It was a Democratic president — and I think we should give Democratic presidents their due on those occasions when they've earned it — that faced his fist in the direction of the Communist world after the crisis in Cuba and said, "If necessary we'll go it alone." But this country is not going to give way to international blackmail and it is precisely the willingness of Republicans and Democrats to be both idealistic and responsible that has contributed to what security is now enjoyed by such nations of the world . . .

Vidal: May I take it would you indeed like us to go to war over Czechoslovakia?

Buckley: Ha-ha. The point is that there wouldn't have been a Czechoslovakian crisis if I had been consulted 25 years ago, Mr. Vidal.

Vidal: But we are consulting you now, Bill.

Buckley: The whole purpose of statesmanship is to abort crisis. You specialize in looking crises in the face and saying irrelevant things about how impossible it is to do anything about [them]. The Republicans specialize in avoiding crises.

Vidal: Oh, they do indeed?

Buckley: Yep.

(crosstalk)

Buckley: Have you noticed that we haven't had any major wars when the Republicans are in? Or have you not done your homework?

Vidal: If I may say so, no thanks to you. Because you, after all, favored the invasion of Cuba, which I understand is still a basic Republican line.

Buckley: The invasion of Cuba, which was undertaken by a Democratic administration, was unfortunately like the defense of Vietnam, something that was done half-way, i.e., it was unsuccessful. I don't believe in (unintelligible).

Vidal: Oh, you don't? Because they're failures.

Buckley: That's right.

Vidal: I must say I don't see any reason why you're not a Democrat because there are many Democrats who enormously agree with you. There is a marvelous quotation of Hubert Humphrey in Saigon, 31st of October 1967, "This is our great adventure and a wonderful one it is." Now that general idea plus the desire to contain Cuba, in your case by force of arms, in our case by . . . I must say the Democrats on one occasion, at the Bay of Pigs, said that they believed in the policy of intervening militarily in the affairs of other countries. I happen to think that that is an immoral and bad idea and that has been the general line of Eugene McCarthy and now Senator [George] McGovern. This to me is the great debate of this convention. It will certainly all stop by Monday . . .

Buckley: It is no doubt a debate and it is certainly one considering which there are differences in rank of both parties, but I do think that Senator McCarthy did himself lasting damage by his total insouciance to what happened in Czechoslovakia. "Oh," said he, "if I had been President I'd have had a couple of extra glasses of ice tea and thought about it tomorrow. Really there was no particular crisis." The crisis of Czechoslovakia precisely is the falling apart of the democratic aspirations of the politics of convergence. It shows that the Soviet Union is still there, still cares naught for world opinion and is still going to press for its old recidivist imperialism.

Vidal: I think it's safe to say that they are behaving as stupidly as we've been behaving in Vietnam. You cannot expect a moratorium on stupidity on the part of empires. I would say to Senator McCarthy, I wish he had put the thing more tactfully, but one of the rather nice things about him is his sometimes cruel accuracy. Since the President was not about to launch an invasion or an attack upon the Soviets, he said, "Why go to all this melodrama when indeed we are not going to do anything?" Oh, you like the melodrama?

Buckley: The reason why, Mr. Vidal, is because there is among decent men (Buckley glances tellingly at Vidal) a tradition that dates back to the Declaration of Independence in which the people who founded this country say that we have a concern for the decent opinion of mankind and the decent opinion of mankind should have been mobilized five minutes after the Czechoslovakian thing . . .

Vidal: (voice rises higher in pitch) To what end? (more calmly) To what end?

Buckley: . . . to use whatever means are at our disposal to create pressure on the Soviet Union. If you think that we are not in a position to damage the Soviet Union you know less about international politics than even I supposed. The Soviet Union, for instance, is constantly running out of things like wheat and we make it possible . . . we and Canada and Australia, for them to have wheat . . .

Vidal: As a matter of fact they've had an extremely good harvest and are on rather secure ground. We have lost the opinion, if you're talking about good opinion . . .

Buckley: No.

Vidal: . . . of all decent men, we have lost the good opinion of all decent men . . .

Buckley: No.

Vidal: . . . in Europe, most of our traditional allies, of Canada who is selling wheat to our enemy . . .

Howard K. Smith: We have about 20 seconds.

(heavy crosstalk)

Vidal: We've lost in Vietnam and now you want us to regain it by going to war in Czechoslovakia.

Buckley: And it is also true that some people lose respect for you precisely at the moment when you should be earning their respect.

Howard K. Smith: I'm terribly sorry, but I have to interrupt you, but we'll continue tomorrow night, and I hope we can get to the Vietnam plank in the Democratic platform.

Debate Eight — Democratic Convention
Sunday, August 25, 1968
Chicago, Illinois
(One day prior to convention)

William F. Buckley Jr.: The tension here at Chicago has something to do with the intuitive knowledge that the candidate the people want is most probably the candidate the people shouldn't indulge themselves. A lot of them know it, but it's going to make a lot of people unhappy.

Gore Vidal: At Miami Beach the people wanted Rockefeller, but the politicians wanted Nixon. Here in Chicago the people want McCarthy, but the politicians seem to want Humphrey. On Wednesday night we shall discover just how democratic the two political parties are.

Howard K. Smith: Not in many years has there been so much criticism as there is now of the convention as an institution and of its end result, a Republican candidate and a Democratic front-runner who are said to arouse little of the enthusiasm that naming a chief executive should involve. I would like to ask our guest commentators is this, the convention, any way to choose a president? The commentators, Gore Vidal, author and once Democratic candidate for Congress in New York, and William Buckley, editor and one-time Conservative candidate for mayor of New York. First, Mr. Buckley.

Buckley: Well, I think, Mr. Smith, that the criticisms of the convention tend to reflect less on abstract complaint than the fact that they happen not to be going the particular way that this particular critic would like. For instance, Mr. Vidal saying a moment ago that the people in Miami Beach wanted Rockefeller rather than Nixon happens among other things, to be false. There was only a single poll that showed Mr. Rockefeller ahead of Mr. Nixon. And, in any case, it was a Republican not a Democratic convention, and every single poll showed Mr. Nixon *way* ahead of Mr. Rockefeller, not only among Republicans, but also among independents. Now what's happening here in Chicago is this. That enough people are tuning in to the realities to recognize that Gene McCarthy is a very attractive man, but he's just a little bit out of this world. And the question is, do we want somebody out of this world to be President of the United States? They decided no in the case of Adlai Stevenson, who was a fusion between organizational and popular enthusiasm in 1952 and was soundly, and I think wisely, defeated for the presidency.

Vidal: Well, I should say to that, first to answer Mr. Buckley's spontaneous inaccuracy, you have almost a Stalinist desire to revise history . . .

Buckley: It wasn't spontaneous. It was planned.

Vidal: I think your calculated desire — Harris and Gallup [Polls] both agreed that Rockefeller was indeed ahead and this was the background to the Republican nominating process in Miami Beach, as we both witnessed, you with more pleasure than I. I would say, to get back to the serious question, if you don't mind, that I don't know if people in the country know or care exactly how undemocratic these conventions are, Republican and Democrat. First, if you want to get on ethnic representation, which is a matter of some importance, 11 percent of the country are black. Here in Chicago, 4 percent of the delegates are black. Four years ago it was 2 percent, so that's some — that is an improvement. Miami Beach 2.2 percent were black. I don't think — so it is not ethnically represented. Now, when you talk about even politically 25 percent of the people at this convention were chosen in 1964 and 1966, so they aren't even plugged in to what were the problems of the day, and by the way 371.5 of Humphrey's votes come from that group which were chosen two and four years ago. And I think all in all — and then they talk about the primaries. Hubert Humphrey said in *The Making of the President*, "Anyone who goes in the primaries is absolutely out of his mind." He's quite right. Only in six states, if you go into a primary and you win the primary, only in six states are the delegates bound by the results. Eight other states they can do whatever they choose. So in a sense, what we have here is political managers have got together. They select the politicians who come together. They do not necessarily represent any people but a series of factions and interests, and I think that time after time they come up with the wrong man, and I think the people are sick of it.

Buckley: Well, I think that Mr. Vidal puts his finger on it when he says that he believes they've come up with the wrong man. Now, the Republicans managed to survive his displeasure and is likely to do so again. The point of the fact is that John Kennedy, for instance, won the primaries and went on to win the convention. Adlai Stevenson was imposed on the convention [in] 1952. He became the heartthrob of all the intellectuals, but he lost to Dwight Eisenhower. The good guys lose, too. My man, [Robert] Taft, who I don't think anybody would seriously contend was less well-equipped than Wendell Willkie to be president, was repudiated by the affirmation of the populace in a sort of a bleacher demonstration. We don't have a perfect democracy and shouldn't have because if you succeeded in achieving it, it would last about two years. We have rather a democracy mediated through institutional arrangements of a sort that keep us from having a kind of plebiscitary democracy which, after all, would relieve us of conventions. All we would have to do is turn our votes over to George Gallop to announce every morning who should occupy the White House. We don't have this and shouldn't have and wise people ought to accept the fact.

Vidal: Well, it is the greater wisdom finally to trust the people and, in any case, we are trusting the people. Just the major politicians are entirely dominated by what the polls say as we witnessed at Miami Beach. They are much influenced. The serious issue here . . .

Buckley: I thought you said they weren't influenced in Miami Beach.

Vidal: The serious issue here is, of course, the idea of direct primaries. Now, I think that the people in the United States, state-by-state, party-by-party, there should be one vote per person. They should vote for the person of their choice, not have it foisted upon them. I remember when I was a delegate from New York State I was selected by the machinery of the state. Carmine DeSapio and a few others picked us because they happened to suspect we'd be for Kennedy in 1960. Shows, in a sense, their good judgment, and it shows the total un-democracy, may I say, of this tactic.

And I think that either this must change, or you are going to see the withering away of the two major parties. I think George Wallace may be the hero in this particular year because he's going to polarize the two parties between right and left. They've got a party of the right. Now we'll have a party of the left.

Howard K. Smith: Wouldn't primaries in all 50 states make elections frightfully expensive, much more than they are now?

Vidal: I think you'd have to change the whole system of elections. I think you might confine, as the British system does, the four weeks of campaigning before the primaries.

Between the primaries and the election another four weeks.
I'd also like to see television time given free to a wide range of
candidates, after all the networks make a good deal of money
on their licenses. They could sacrifice eight weeks of prime
time for democracy in action. If you did this you would cut
down . . .

Buckley: (inaudible)

Vidal: If you did, you could cut down the cost of elections by
many, many millions of dollars and you might have a more
interesting array of candidates than we do this year.

Howard K. Smith: What about the matter of enthusiasm for
the candidates? Does it have to be wild in order for a candidate to be a good president?

Buckley: The factor I think to keep one's eyes on there is that
inevitably enthusiasm accumulates for redemptorists. People
who view the world, view the universe, and say, "You have
only to elect me and I will achieve paradise on earth." There
is, however fortunately, a conservative instinct among the
people that smells the baloney in these arguments, and you
see this working paradoxically here in Chicago where for all of
his charm, for all of his spontaneity, for all of his otherworld-
liness people are recognizing that Gene McCarthy would be
a catastrophic President of the United States. And sometimes
it seems almost as though it would be worthwhile to have
a catastrophic president simply for the aesthetic pleasure of

hearing him recite his elegies over what is happening under his stewardship, but sometimes people figure, well, probably they ought to get their kicks in other ways.

Vidal: I think this is the first time I've ever heard you come out against the aesthetics of politics. I always thought you liked the idea of politics as a rather remote sense of affairs.

Buckley: Kept in their place, kept in their place. I never found Robert Taft an aesthetically pleasing politician.

Vidal: Did you not?

Buckley: But I certainly think he should have been president again and again and again, however democratic he is . . .

Vidal: He was not and was not and was not.

Buckley: I know.

Vidal: But at the same time . . .

Buckley: I know.

Vidal: I think McCarthy is plainly the choice of a majority of the people according to the polls to the extent that we want to pay any attention to them. I think that the polls are useful and . . .

Buckley: Not on that plane. He never got a majority in any state he ever ran in. Do you recognize that?

Vidal: Oh, indeed I do. As a matter of fact he did — then why did you say that? You're absolutely wrong.

(much inaudible crosstalk)

Vidal: He won the thing, absolutely.

Buckley: He didn't win a majority. Do you understand what I'm saying?

Vidal: Of course I do. Plurality.

Buckley: Alright.

Vidal: Isn't that what you see him do?

Buckley: Do you want to change the majority of plurality?

Vidal: No, indeed I'm not.

Buckley: Thirty-three percent can win plurality.

Vidal: You are wrong again.

Howard K. Smith: Can we freeze this argument . . .

Vidal: I'm sorry, there are many children watching.

Howard K. Smith: . . . in a state of suspension? We'll come back to it tomorrow. Thank you very much indeed, gentlemen. We'll be looking forward to your observations every night of the convention.

Monday, August 26, 1968
(First day of convention)

Editor's Note: For reasons that are not clear, Buckley and Vidal did not debate on the opening day of the Democratic National Convention.

Debate Nine — Democratic Convention
Tuesday, August 27, 1968
Chicago, Illinois
(Second day of convention)

William F. Buckley Jr.: Well, the Vietnam plank, as it finally emerged, signifies the victory of nerves over panic, of strategic humanitarianism over temporary profit, of the survival by idealism of the wastebasket.

Gore Vidal: Today the McCarthy/McGovern peace forces were defeated in the platform committee by the Johnson/ Humphrey majority and tonight a majority of the delegates will also show their appreciation of the President's masterly conduct of his Asiatic war. Fortunately, platforms are not made for action, but for the wastebasket.

Howard K. Smith: The main source of contention on the floor of the convention tonight is the Vietnam plank of the newly published Democratic platform. I would like to ask our guest commentators if they can find any serious differences between what the Republicans said about Vietnam and what the Democrats say about it. To my mind I see very little difference. Our guests are the playwright, Gore Vidal, a Democrat, a former candidate for Congress from New York State, and William Buckley, editor, and a former candidate for mayor of New York City. Mr. Buckley, will you begin?

Buckley: I think that the important difference, Mr. Smith, is not in the planks as they were finally written, but in the effort that went into their composition. The Democrats, a great many of them, are clearly displeased with the plank insofar as it doesn't call immediately for an unconditional end in bombing. We know that Mr. McGovern and Mr. McCarthy joined forces to demand nothing less than that, the unconditional end of bombing. There were no equivalent forces in the Republican Party for that, although they ended up saying, roughly, the same thing. One is entitled to suppose that in the case of the Republicans, this truly represents the settlement of the overwhelming majority of them, which is not the case concerning the Democrats.

Vidal: I think that's well-observed. There's a definite split here tonight. I personally favored, as many people did, the McCarthy/McGovern plank. I was just told the latest hot rumor here at the convention hall that the plank was given to Lyndon B. Johnson himself who rewrote it and sent it back and that is the one that they are now celebrating down on the floor. We were just given bits and pieces of this platform and my favorite little bit here is: "We strongly support the Paris talks and applaud the initiative of President Johnson which brought

North Vietnam to the peace table." Of course, it was Senator McCarthy in New Hampshire and the enormous movement of a great many people in the United States that caused our leader to make that diplomatic gesture. So I would say that the difference between the two platforms is, as Mr. Buckley suggests, the Republicans are pretty united in being not only on the one hand hawkish, but on the other hand, they seem to feel that they are open for negotiation trying to relive, I suppose, the days of the Korean settlement by General Eisenhower who talked very tough in the campaign and then, of course, made a peace with Korea. I suspect that may well be the Nixon plan. Meanwhile, you have a very divided Democratic Party here tonight.

Howard K. Smith: What can the Republicans do that the Democrats can't if Nixon is elected, Mr. Buckley?

Buckley: Well, if Nixon is elected it seems to me that (video glitch) the strategic seriousness of our anti-Communist position there, that is to say that he won't be hampered by a divided party, some of which, perhaps even a majority of which, is bitterly opposed, as Mr. Vidal quite correctly suggests, to this policy. I do think, though, that Mr. Vidal's diagnosis is insufficient primarily for the reason that he doesn't take into account extremes of circumstances. For instance Eisenhower's peace on Korea may very well, as Democratic Chairman Paul Butler pointed out at the time, have also had something to do with the death of [Joseph] Stalin which conveniently took place two or three months after Eisenhower's election. But also one has to bear in mind that there have been such sentimentalities as calling for a coalition government, that's calling for sending blood to the Vietcong, all that kind of business which have considerably hampered the negotiations which might otherwise have taken place more speedily.

Vidal: Well, I think Mr. Buckley has given us a preview of what we will hear from the Republicans on this subject. I'd like to introduce a note that absolutely nobody has so far in the Vietnam debate. That is that I happen to favor sort of diplomacy in the grand old style. I'm sure Mr. Buckley will agree with me since he, too, is a lover of the Congress of Vienna and Metternich policy. That we should, since Ho Chi Minh is the enemy of Mao Tse-tung, therefore, we should support Ho Chi Minh. Mao Tse-tung is the enemy of the Kremlin, therefore, in certain cases we should support him, and the Kremlin is, of course, the enemy of Mao Tse-tung and we should support them. Now this is grand politics. This is not ideological. It's not as interesting as a holy war, that is a fascinating war that we are the forces of light and we must destroy all other governments. But it has always been traditional in the conduct of foreign policy until the pietisms of John Foster Dulles, who really did believe, at least as far as well can tell, that we were indeed the forces of light and they were night, that we began forcing our way into the world and forever setting up this pietistic view that governments we disapproved of should be dealt with harshly. I'm simply saying to the extent that the leader of North Vietnam is no friend of China, this is not a monolithic conspiracy, we should support him, and by the same token Mao Tse-tung and again in this Viennese Congressional circle. Mr. Buckley, would you like to add to that?

Buckley: Mr. Vidal's suggestion that perhaps it would be in our interest to support Ho Chi Minh suggests perhaps also that as a matter of testamentary integrity I reveal a concrete proposal to that end contained in a letter sent to me by Senator [Robert] Kennedy about six months ago, the P.S. of which was: "I have changed my platform for 1968 from 'Let's give blood to the Vietcong' to 'Let's give Gore Vidal to the Vietcong.'" (Buckley produces letter from pocket inside his suit jacket.)

Vidal: May I see that? Really? (Buckley hands letter to Vidal.)

Buckley: I think, however, that would be immoderate. In any case, I do share Mr. Kennedy's notion that Mr. Vidal's idea of how to prosecute the whole situation out there, quite apart from the fact of a congruence of general policy, is marred by his sort of strange fantasies concerning the realisms of politics.

Vidal: I must say, I am looking at this. What a very curious handwriting. It also slants up, a sign of a manic depressive.

Buckley: Did you say that about Senator Kennedy?

Vidal: I did say that. Whether you forged it or not, I don't know (laughter). I will have to have my handwriting experts, the graphologists will have to look at it. I put nothing beyond you, not since the Dreyfus case when we had such evidence brought into court. But it's very, very amusing and has nothing to do with the case. The fact that he was writing you letters makes me terribly suspicious of him as a presidential candidate. I will say that . . .

Buckley: This is Senator *Bobby* Kennedy.

Vidal: Yes, I realize that. I recognize the handwriting. (crosstalk) Makes me very suspicious of what he might have been like as President. But to get back to the plank — it's been fun inspecting your correspondence. But what matters here is that we have, in a word, lost the war. And I think that that was really the impression that the McCarthy/Mc-Govern people have been trying to give the country. That we must get out of this. It's cost us 100 billion dollars. It's cost us 25,000 dead. Something like 90 percent of the casualties are civilian, so when they accuse us of genocide they are not without a point.

Buckley: Now wait a minute . . .

Vidal: We have nothing to gain by this war.

Buckley: Now wait a minute . . . the activity of the United States in North Vietnam cannot be categorized as genocide by anyone who doesn't accept the postulates of the Communist Party, their postulates being, of course, that we are interested in killing people for the sake of killing people. The distinction being, how many people is it necessary to kill in order to pursue a perfectly legitimate military mission, a distinction that has been honored during the past thousand years? We have not lost the war in Vietnam. What we have lost is an opportunity to press that war with such weapons as are especially at our disposal and the reason we haven't is because we have proceeded schizophrenically — make love to the Communists this side of the hemisphere, hate 'em and kill 'em this side of the hemisphere . . .

Vidal: Do you favor just an all-out war on communism?

Buckley: No . . .

Vidal: . . . to use nuclear weapons as you have [suggested] in the past on the Chinese nuclear capacity?

(crosstalk)

Vidal: Yes, indeed. (more crosstalk) In something marvelous called "A Blow for Peace," you came out, you said, quote, ". . . to give a two-hour notice to the Red Chinese that we intend to destroy these nuclear facilities and so give the civilian and military [a chance] to evacuate the plants which we would then proceed, pure and simple, to blow up." This is the great statesman sitting here on my right. That is an act of war.

Buckley: Why with nuclear weapons? I never said with

nuclear weapons. Blow them up with poison ivy for all I'm concerned. The point is . . .

Vidal: What is the difference? That is an act of war. It is an act of war. To drop bombs on any country is an act of war.

(crosstalk)

Buckley: Mr. Vidal, if you want to change what you finished saying a moment ago I will welcome any change at any point in here. You said a moment ago that I favored nuclear bombing of Red China. For the record I did not. I favored, alongside a number of . . . very serious military strategists, a preemptive strike against the nuclear facilities of Red China . . .

Vidal: And you expect to be taken seriously?

Buckley: . . . a position which was explored by President John F. Kennedy in the fall of 1963 and should be thought of by all serious people who not only are against the nuclear bomb in the café society sense . . .

Vidal: My dear Mr. Buckley. . .

Buckley: . . . but try to do something about it. If the bad guys have got the nuclear bomb [then] you both have it.

Howard K. Smith: You are both much better when you don't talk at the same time. Could we take turns?

(crosstalk)

Vidal: I would like to pick up that point. You did indeed want to drop bombs on China, which is a foreign country of enormous size. It is no business of ours, I should think, to give them a Pearl Harbor. You have also advocated the invasion of Cuba in what you called the immediate enactment of the Monroe Doctrine, something I suspect you have never read because the Monroe Doctrine ceased to exist, in fact, since 1917. [The] Monroe Doctrine, for your information, happened to have been dependent upon foreign powers . . . the United States, in this hemisphere, were not to be allowed, but by the same token we would maintain ourselves outside European affairs. We abrogated that by going into the First World War. So, in effect, the Monroe Doctrine does not exist, in this case.

Buckley: Mr. Vidal, it is a laborious job to straighten out history after you've had a couple of sentences' go at it. The distinction was that we would not go to Europe except at the invitation of Europe. If you will give me the name of one country in Europe where we are without the invitation of the local government, then I will say that we have violated the equivalent of the Monroe Doctrine . . .

(crosstalk)

Howard K. Smith: (interrupts) The discussion is about the plank in Vietnam. How do we get out? Have we really been beaten?

Buckley: The answer is that we have not been beaten, Mr. Smith. The answer is that we are negotiating in Paris at this moment because the enemy feels the pressure of a four, five year effort by the United States and South Vietnam and certain of its Asian allies. It's not there simply because Senator McCarthy got 43,000 votes in New Hampshire. This isn't the way Haiphong works . . . Hanoi works. We can, of course, win the war, but it's going to take our concerted effort, and it's going to take the kind of (video glitch) lazily incapable of generating as a result of the kind of erosion of purpose to which people like Mr. Vidal contribute, sometimes eloquently, sometimes not.

Vidal: I still don't see how Mr. Buckley, with his concerted will, thinks that we're going to win a war that we have spent certainly five very aggressive years in losing. We have tried search and destroy. We have dropped more bombs on it than we dropped on Europe in the Second World War. We are getting absolutely nowhere. They have the perfect desire to organize their own country in their own way and there is no problem about. We are in the presence, however, if I may say so, of, I would suspect, the most war-minded person in the United States. And usually Mr. Buckley doesn't reveal himself as clearly as he has tonight. But, indeed, he has come out for a preemptive strike against Red China [which is an] act of war . . .

Buckley: In 1963 . . .

Vidal: No, you came out for it 1964, December 29th in *National Review.* You do write your own columns, don't you?

Buckley: I said, Mr. Kennedy in 1963 and I came out in 1964. I *considered* it in '63.

Vidal: There's a difference between consideration and proposing it.

Buckley: The point is, Mr. Vidal, that there are those people who are always deploring what ought to have been done back when certain other people were saying it should have been done at that moment. Now, one of these days you're going to sit around shaking and talking about better red than dead because Red China has a hydrogen bomb. And the answer will be who was it who a few years ago thought that might have been the time, as for instance in Munich, to stop appeasement? I don't say that life is going to be completely easy, completely non-dangerous . . . there are bad people in this world.

Vidal: I know you are interested in Munich and interested in the past. And, of course, every decision you would have made correctly had you been asked . . .

(crosstalk)

Vidal: . . . somehow the good judgment of the country maintained itself. (more crosstalk) And here we are today and you are talking in the vaguest of terms saying now we are going to win in Vietnam. Now I assume . . .

Buckley: I said we *could* win . . . I didn't say we were going to.

Vidal: You said we *will* win . . .

Buckley: (emphatically) I said we *could*, Mr. Vidal.

Vidal: Could we or *should* we?

Buckley: (stated laconically for comic effect) Oh well, obviously, we should.

Vidal: A-ha. Well, that's all we needed to know. Here he sits, take a good look at the leading warmonger in the United States. Bill, don't you point your tongue at me now. Keep it in your cheek where it belongs.

Buckley: If I am the leading warmonger in the United States then I am to be contrasted with you in the sense in which the majority of people of the United States, including the leadership of the Democratic Party and the leadership of the Republican Party, belong with me while you go to Rome and expatriate yourself . . .

Vidal: I think we can straighten this out now. I don't expatriate myself. I have an apartment in Rome and I go there for two or three months every year to be close to the Vatican to

contemplate William Buckley and his mad activities back here
... (a pipe or prop on the set drops loudly to the floor) with
enormous serenity. They're trying to get us, Bill.

Buckley: Yes ... (quickly getting back to the debate) ... And
you published in January of this year in a book the following
statement: "Unless the war in Vietnam is renounced by the
next elected President of the United States, I see no moral
alternative than to renounce my citizenship, dash, Vidal." We
may not have anything to lose at the end of this election.

Vidal: It may very well be that all (unintelligible). I must say
it must be mysterious to you to find somebody acting out of
a moral principle. But after all, sooner or later we must all be
confronted with these Thomas More decisions and I'm sure
that you will settle for Wales and I for the block.

Buckley: The encyclopedia of morality which constitutes your
published work is hardly my primary source.

Vidal: Do you read?

Howard K. Smith: Mr. Vidal, would it have been possible for
any other president to have behaved differently in a decisive
way from the way President Johnson did, say, in 1965? We
have two ex-presidents, one a Republican, one a Democrat,
who both say he's right. The dead president said two months
before his death that he believed in the Domino Theory and felt
that we should not let South Vietnam fall to the Communists.

Vidal: I have a strange feeling that empires have their own built-in dynamism. And you may be right that with the kind of presidents that we tend to have now reflect the mood of the country. It may very well be that the empire of ours that has been going on since 1899 when we picked "Remember the Maine," which was as phony as the Tonkin Gulf Resolution. We've been in the empire business since 1899. We picked a war with Spain. We ended up with the Philippines, which we then liberated against their will and added to our empire. We became a great Pacific power. We tried an invasion of Canada . . .

Buckley: [Are you giving us] all of history?

Vidal: You could learn a great deal.

Buckley: I know, but not on public time.

Vidal: . . . and at the end of it, we are now on the mainland of Asia. I think, to be perfectly bleak and to be perfectly blunt, I think we are headed for total disaster, this empire, with people like Mr. Buckley here beating the drum. And I think, the instinct of the people, I used to think, was for peace. Now I come back and I see little American flags on the antennae of the car . . . they are getting ready for war. They are getting ready for war. I think probably Lyndon Johnson is simply an agent of nature. That the empire is getting to a point where there is going to be a blow up [due to] overpopulation. The ecological balance of the planet is upset. The food supply is in danger. I think there is war coming.

Buckley: Mr. Smith, this is a recurrent phenomenon. People like to sort of massage their world-weariness and tell us how everything is going to the dogs. There's a curious coincidence about the fact that it's always going to the dogs because we don't do what they tell us to do. I don't know how robust America is, but I'm sure it's robust enough to survive crises in the future. I don't remember any time during the past 20 years when we haven't heard the scare talk America has about six months left to go. The answer is that we have, I think, more than that left to go, though I do think there are times to worry about. But a collection of that kind [of] syndrome is there (Buckley points to Vidal), not in the Democratic platform of tonight.

Vidal: I must say, six months to go . . . Richard Nixon was the last person to do that in the nineteen, (rolls eyes upward to think) . . . 1956 election. (imitating Nixon's voice) "We have one month to save America," said Richard Nixon.

Buckley: And we saved it, didn't we?

Vidal: We got Eisenhower whom you highly disapproved of . . .

Buckley: How do you know we wouldn't have saved it if we hadn't voted for Eisenhower?

Vidal: Ha-ha. Were we saved?

Howard K. Smith: Let me ask you about another part of the Democratic platform which isn't being debated. The Democrats are in favor of law and justice where the Republicans are in favor of law and order. Is there any distinction?

Buckley: There is a metaphysical distinction which I'm sure has not been observed by the people who formulated the policies. A state as defined in the liberal idea is not a state which accepts justice as its primary goal for the reason that elementary distinctions were made millennia ago between the city of God and the city of Man. Granted the rhetoric of the Democratic Party sometimes seems to give us the impression that it is ushering in the city of God, except that God is unconstitutional. Given that, it seems to be trying to go in that direction. The Republican emphasis on law and order is, in my judgment, perhaps for accidental reasons, in closer congruity to the limited aspirations of a constitution of a free republic.

Vidal: I think Mr. Buckley has very fairly stated, as usual, the viewpoint of the Daughters of the American Revolution. In actual fact the Democratic Party is a little bit ahead of the Republican Party on this particular issue. The metaphysical point, as Mr. Buckley would say, really is between what do you think about having a strong federal government as opposed to a strong local government?, and this is a legitimate and a continuing debate. I would only give you this reminder:

That without a strong federal government no school would have even begun to be integrated in the South. There never would have been a Pure Drug and Food Act. While we were down there in Miami I noticed that the . . . what was it? . . . the Florida power and light company was going to put an atomic reactor in Biscayne Bay which would have cooked all the fish. The local chamber of commerce thought this was a marvelous idea. Anything for money, and the Department of the Interior stopped it. Mr. Buckley, with his *laissez faire* love of doing business in the United States — anything that makes money has to be good; that's American — probably would have allowed this. I say that the federal government must act in certain great issues . . .

Buckley: Did you follow that one, Mr. Smith? That sounds like one of those orators out there. However, I'll transcribe it and study it.

Vidal: No, I think . . .

Buckley: I'm in favor of killing sharks in Biscayne Bay for profit, is that right?

(crosstalk)

Vidal: Oh Bill, Bill, your people are . . . the terrible thing about it is that absolutely nothing would ever be done at the local level. You think there would be one integrated school in the South without the Supreme Court decision?

Buckley: Before we had a strong central government we had a civil war the purpose of which was to free the slaves. So I think that good things can happen even without the federal government . . .

Vidal: That's an irrelevant comment.

Buckley: . . . a federal government which incidentally all of the Democrats should be apologizing for at this moment. You may have noticed in the platform that they're all saying we've got to retreat — as Senator Kennedy was saying — we've got to retreat from the idea that the federal government can do everything. (crosstalk) This is something we conservatives have been saying for quite a while.

Vidal: As a matter of fact this year's liberal rhetoric has fallen into a conservative chapter. We must get private enterprise, that great machine of American virtue, as Richard Nixon said, "This alone can help us in the ghettos with the Negroes." Well, private enterprise won't. They'll get the tax cut he promises, and that'll be the last we hear because they are there to make money, not . . .

Buckley: Don't you understand, Mr. Vidal, that the making of money is, according to systems discovered 300 years ago as the beginning of economic liberty, a way of helping people because it is a way of making goods available to people at a cheaper price. Henry Ford made a lot of money, but he also reduced the price of cars from 5,000 dollars to 500 bucks. Got it? Got it?

Howard K. Smith: I think this is the last remark. Can you do it in one line?

Vidal: Yes, simply in one line, it has been a great pleasure to observe America's leading hawk and great heart with his enormous compassion — don't stick your tongue out, Bill — once again in action.

Howard K. Smith: That was a long line. We must break it off there and we will continue tomorrow night.

Debate Ten — Democratic Convention
Wednesday, August 28, 1968
Chicago, Illinois
(Third day of convention)

Editor's Note: This, the penultimate debate between Buckley and Vidal, is arguably the most infamous televised debate of the last half-century. Those who remember the debates from 1968 typically fixate on the name-calling that ensued after heated rhetoric that escalated, or sank in some opinions, to language that was not allowed on the public airwaves. To understand precisely what happened and how things nearly came to fisticuffs, some background information is necessary and has not been sufficiently reported previously. Outside the convention center, police were nearly in full-scale riot against demonstrators. Many innocent bystanders, including journalists covering the convention, were savagely beaten. Tear gas was not only clouding the streets outside the convention center, but had leaked inside as well, causing much misery among the newsmen and technicians from the networks. Vidal, who vainly declined to wear his eyeglasses except when absolutely necessary, was forced to wear them on camera this particular evening because his eyes were tearing-up too much to read without them.

Buckley had a fall on his yacht that fractured his collarbone one day before he was to report for duty in Miami Beach for the first debate. Off-camera he wore a clavicle brace, but carefully hid the injury in the studio, even though he was reportedly in a great deal of pain. (In the video, as the name-calling reaches its highest pitch, Buckley leans forward menacingly and seems ready to throw the first punch. At the precise moment physical violence seems a real possibility, Buckley abruptly falls back into his chair, signaling that he doesn't intend to take things further. It is believed that the forward motion by Buckley possibly resulted in an intense jolt of pain in his collarbone area, sidelining him from any physical remonstration. As writer James Wolcott coolly observed, Vidal didn't flinch.) Further, family members confirm that Buckley had sleep difficulties. He was kept awake, as he states, by demonstrators throughout the previous night. This sleep deprivation did not make him merely more tired, it had an effect on his entire mood, setting the fuse for an outburst he clearly later regretted.

The circumstances on the street had everyone in the studio on edge and anxious. Vidal, for his part, was angry at the police. They were responsible for the tear gas. Buckley was angry at the demonstrators, who caused him to lose precious sleep and in his mind provoked the police. Taking these issues into consideration, heightened anger and rhetoric were all but inevitable. And Vidal's parting words to Buckley when it was all over?: "Well, I guess we gave them their money's worth tonight."

Howard K. Smith: (video begins with Smith in mid-conversation) . . . and to our two guest commentators, William Buckley and Gore Vidal, and to ask them what observations they've made about the security that we have seen all week at this convention and the events tonight on the streets beyond this convention hall. Who is first? Mr. Vidal, first.

Gore Vidal: I think there is very little that we can say after those pictures that would be in any way adequate. [**Editor's Note:** Vidal is referring to graphic video footage of the police clashing with demonstrators that was aired just prior to the debates.] It's like living under a Soviet regime here. The guards, the soldiers, the *agents provocateur* on the parts of the police. You've seen the roughing up. The background of it is that they came here for a rally on the 25th of August at Soldier Field, a coalition for an open convention. They were denied the use of the field. It was a friendly, nonviolent demonstration. As a rule the press is on the side of the police. But this time the police have seriously injured some 21 newsmen, and the press has, of course, reacted, and on top of that television is duly upset with Mayor [Richard J.] Daley for other reasons. I'd like to point out, picking up a newspaper at random on my way here, *The Chicago Daily News*, and a columnist called Mike Royko, who says, "Thomas E. Ferran, the U.S. Attorney, says 'Chicago police have shown, quote, wonderful discipline in their handling of the Lincoln Park demonstrators.' Ferran is either stupid or a liar or maybe he's been wandering around in the wrong park. Chicago's police, for his information, have been beating innocent people with, to coin a phrase, reckless abandon." And he goes on to say, "The biggest threat to law and order in the last week has been the Chicago Police Department." On an inside page here we have one of the grisliest pictures I have seen in some time. It shows a group of police standing and laughing as they have thrown into the water a young man on a bicycle. And the caption is: "The witnesses said the police then just stood back and laughed. The youth reportedly had just been riding through the park, he had not even been a part of the Yippie gathering."

Howard K. Smith: I wonder if we can let Mr. Buckley comment now for a short while?

William F. Buckley Jr.: The distinctions to be made, Mr. Smith, are these: Number One, do we have enough evidence to indict a large number of individual Chicago policemen? It would seem from what Mr. Burns showed us [**Editor's Note:** Buckley is referring to ABC's video footage.] that we do. However, the effort here — not only on your program tonight, but during the past two or three days in Chicago — has been to institutionalize this complaint so as to march forward and say that, in effect, we have got a police state going here, we have got a sort of a fascist situation.

One young man approached me, last night, and said, "Are you aware that Mayor Daley is a fascist?" — to which my reply was, "No. And if that is the case, why didn't John Kennedy and Bobby Kennedy, whose favorite mayor he was, indict him as such, and teach us that we should all despise him as a fascist?"

The point is that policemen violate their obligations just the way politicians do. (voice rises in anger) If we could all work up an equal sweat, and if you all would be obliging enough to have your cameras handy every time a politician commits demagogy or passes along graft or bribes, or every time a businessman cheats on his taxes, or every time a labor union beats up people who refuse to join his union — then maybe we could work up some kind of impartiality in resentment. As of this moment, I say: go after those cops who were guilty of unnecessary brutality [and] develop your doctrine of security sufficiently so that when you don't have as many cops as you should have had — for instance, in Dallas, in November of 1963 — you don't [then] go and criticize the FBI for not having been there, for not having taken sufficient security measures. But don't do what's happening here in Chicago tonight, which is to infer from individual and despicable acts of violence, a case for implicit totalitarianism in the American system.

Howard K. Smith: Mr. Vidal.

Vidal: I should say that the issue was, of course, go after the bad cops. There are good cops as well as bad. But there is a more important issue here, a constitutional issue and this is going to be repeated across the country. We have the right, according to our Constitution, of freedom of assembly. And if you want to hold a meeting for a peaceful purpose to demonstrate, you have that right. That right was abrogated by Mayor Daley, by his administration, by the Cook County sheriff, Joseph Woods. These people came here with no desire other than anybody's ever been able to prove, than to hold peaceful demonstrations.

Buckley: I can prove it.

Vidal: How can you prove it?

Buckley: Very easily. By citing the recorded words of Mr. [Tom] Hayden of the SDS, of Mr. Rennie Davis of the Co-ordinating Committee — whose object has been to, quote, "break down the false and deceptive institutions of bourgeois democracy sufficient to send in a revolutionary order." Anybody who believes that these characters are interested in the democratic process is deluding himself. I was 14 windows above that gang last night . . . these sweet little girls with their sun-baked dresses that we heard described a moment ago, and the chant between 11 o'clock and 5 o'clock this morning, some four or five thousand voices, was sheer, utter obscenities directed at the President of the United States, at the mayor of this city, plus also the intermittent refrain, quote, "Ho Ho Ho/ Ho Chi Minh/The NLF/is sure to win!"

This is their way of accosting American society concerning their brothers, their sisters, their uncles, their fathers, who are being shot at by an enemy, which wrongly or rightly nevertheless we are fighting. I say it is remarkable that there was as much restraint shown as was shown, for instance, last night by cops who were out there for 17 hours without inflicting a single wound on a single person even though that kind of disgusting stuff was being thrown at them and at all of American society.

Howard K. Smith: Our reporter, Jim Burns, said there ought to be a different way to handle situations like that.

Buckley: (leans forward in seat and responds to Smith heatedly) I wish he would invent it. Why don't you ask him next time — maybe tomorrow — to tell us how to handle it. Because I'm sure the Republican Party and the Democratic Party would [gladly] form a joint platform which would suggest how to do it. Every time we develop an instrument like Mace for instance, the purpose of which is actually to stop a situation when the law is on the side of stopping it without rendering permanent injury, and everybody goes hog mad at its use. What are we, in fact, supposed to use when they break law and order as handed down by judges? Right to assembly is not absolute, the Supreme Court has ruled in several occasions.

Howard K. Smith: Let Mr. Vidal have a chance.

Vidal: The right of assembly is in the Constitution, in the Bill of Rights.

Buckley: (garbled)

Vidal: Nothing on earth is absolute.

Buckley: (garbled)

Vidal: That's right. We live in a relativist world. However, it is the law, it is the Constitution and . . . and let us have no more sly comments in your capacity as the enemy of the people. By the way, you got an invitation this afternoon I haven't passed on to you from Norman Mailer, our mutual friend, who was out there as was I on Monday night. He said, "You tell Buckley to come out here. He might be very interested to see how his beloved police are behaving."

Buckley: I was there.

Vidal: No, you said you were on the 15th floor, I don't believe you were there. And furthermore, when you start quoting Tom Hayden and the other leaders of the New Left who were involved in this, I suggest you get the quotes right. They are talking about revolution. They are not talking about bloody civil war, as you would indicate.

Buckley: Yeah, yeah.

Vidal: Well, until you get the exact quotes . . . you are well known . . . for distortion.

(crosstalk)

Buckley: All you do is violate the law you say . . .

Vidal: (raises voice) It is no violation of the law to freely demonstrate, as you well know.

Buckley: Now wait a minute. The law is not something that you make up.

Vidal: No, it is something in the Constitution that you cannot interpret. They came here for free assembly. They came here to demonstrate against the Vietnam War, which you happen to love. I'm sorry for that. They have not been allowed to hold a meeting in Soldier Field which they should have had, could have had, would have had a peaceful demonstration. (in an increasingly angry tone) Instead, the police fired [up] by Mayor Daley and by a lot of jingoes around here have been roughing up everybody from the press to the delegates to the kids out there, and you want to sit hereby and talk about all that (in a mock Buckley voice) law and order.

Buckley: I'm going to talk to you about what the Supreme Court says, including Oliver Wendell Holmes, whom presumably you also despise. But the first relevant decision 110 years ago says that the demands of rights of assembly are not absolute in the sense that for instance there is no obligation on the part of the city of Chicago to allow all these people to come into this amphitheater and demonstrate. An extension of that piece of common sense shows the wisdom and the correctness of the federal court and the Supreme Court in the past to say that you cannot arrange a demonstration in such a way as to interfere with other people's freedoms. Mr. Burns admitted a moment ago that these people were interrupting the freedoms of people to cross the street for instance.

Vidal: Freedoms of people to cross the street?

Buckley: They weren't given a license to demonstrate . . .

Vidal: At that particular moment. However, when they were in the parks on Monday night, when I observed them, I watched the police come in like this (makes gesture) from all directions, standing. [The demonstrators] were sitting there, singing folk songs. There were none of the obscenities which your ear alone seems to have picked up. They were absolutely well-behaved. Then, suddenly, the police began. You'd see one little stirring up in one corner. Then, you'd suddenly see a bunch of them come in with their nightclubs and, may I say, without their badges, which is illegal . . .

Howard K. Smith: Mr. Vidal, wasn't it a provocative act to try to raise the Vietcong flag in the park, in the film we just saw? Wouldn't that invite — raising a Nazi flag in World War II, would have had similar consequences?

Vidal: You must realize what some of the political issues are here . . .

Buckley: You are so naïve . . .

Vidal: There are many people in the United States [who]

happen to believe that the United States' policy is wrong in Vietnam and the Vietcong are correct in wanting to organize their country in their own way politically. This happens to be pretty much the opinion of Western Europe and many other parts of the world. If it is a novelty in Chicago that is too bad . . . I assume that the point of American democracy is you can express any point of view you want . . ."

Buckley: (garbled)

Vidal: Shut up a minute.

Buckley: No, I won't. Some people are pro-Nazi and the answer is that they were well-treated by people who ostracized them, and I am for ostracizing people who egg on other people to shoot American Marines and American soldiers. I know you don't care . . .

Vidal: As far as I am concerned, the only pro- or crypto-Nazi I can think of is yourself, failing that, I would only say that we can't have . . .

Howard K. Smith: Let's stop calling names . . .

Buckley: (Buckley loses his composure) Now listen, you queer. Stop calling me a crypto-Nazi or I'll sock you in your goddamn face and you'll stay plastered.

Howard K. Smith: Gentlemen! Let's not call names . . .

Vidal: Oh, Bill . . .

Buckley: . . . Let Myra Breckinridge go back to his pornography and stop making any allusions of Nazism . . .

Howard K. Smith: I beg you . . .

Buckley: I was in the infantry in the last war and fought Nazism . . .

Vidal: You were *not* in the infantry. As a matter of fact you didn't fight in the war.

Buckley: I *was* in the infantry.

Vidal: You were not. You're distorting your own military record . . . what happened at Sharon? [**Editor's Note:** Sharon refers to Sharon, Connecticut and a youthful indiscretion of siblings of Mr. Buckley. In the *Esquire* magazine essay Vidal would write in 1969, "A Distasteful Encounter with William F. Buckley Jr.," the so-called "Sharon incident" figures prominently in his attack on Buckley. However, Bill Buckley was not involved in the incident and in fact was serving in the military at the time.]

Howard K. Smith: Mr. Vidal, wasn't it a provocative act to pull down an American flag and put up a Vietcong flag even if you disagree with what the United States is doing?

Vidal: It is *not* a provocative act. You have every right, in this country, to take any position you want to take because we are guaranteed freedom of speech. We've just listened to (Buckley tries to interrupt. Vidal raises his voice to talk over Buckley.) a certainly grotesque example of it.

Howard K. Smith: Now, let's not talk at the same time. Mr. Buckley.

Buckley: Certain acts that are lawful are nevertheless provocative. I'll give you an example. George Lincoln Rockwell wanted to go to Manhattan and stage a "hate Jew" rally, see. Now, Mayor [Robert] Wagner said, "No, you can't." The American Civil Liberties Union said, well, George Lincoln Rockwell has got a right to go there under the Constitution. Theoretically he has the right, but there is no question it would have been provocative. I, for one, have to confess I would have been discreetly on the side of people who threw tomatoes and maybe something even a little tougher at George Lincoln Rockwell. Now here is an example of a right, but nevertheless, as you point out, a provocation. One doesn't go to Manhattan and come out in favor of Buchenwald. I think the whole point of the American system is, and this is something a lot of people don't understand, that the reason we succeed as a society is because we exclude certain things. We exclude genocide, we exclude class hatred, we ought to exclude it. And whether it's fighting a [Lester] Maddox here, or fighting people who come out in favor of Ho Chi Minh in Lincoln Park, the whole purpose of American society is that we are in favor of people who want to be free, not in favor of people who want to despise anybody else or commit America to genocidal policies.

Howard K. Smith: Mr. Vidal?

Vidal: (responds almost hesitantly) What more to say on the subject? I think we've seen enough actions of Mr. Buckley on this issue, the infantry warrior. He never saw a shot fired in anger. I would point out, I come back . . . you keep asking me, Howard, about this provocative act. There are many acts which provoke. If you are going to have freedom of assembly and freedom of speech you must be able to say it. That is the whole point of this country. And once this is abrogated then I think we might just as well stop these wars of freedom. What are we doing fighting in Vietnam if you cannot freely express yourself in the streets of Chicago?

Howard K. Smith: I think we have run out of time, and I thank you very much for the discussion. There was a little more heat and a little less light than usual, but it was still very worth hearing.

Debate Eleven —
Democratic Convention
Thursday, August 29, 1968
Chicago, Illinois
(Fourth and final day of convention)

Editor's Note: In several interviews prior to his death, Vidal insisted that after his infamous blow-up with Buckley in the penultimate debate in Chicago he and Buckley never met face-to-face again. He claimed that ABC News required a curtain be placed between them to reduce any rancor from poisoning their final contracted debate. As can be seen clearly in the video, however, Buckley and Vidal sat literally inches away from one another for the last debate, their knees nearly touching. The body language between them is powerfully telling. Each man tilts away from the other at nearly a 45-degree angle. They do not look at one another or specifically address one another for the entire debate.

The two men had to return to ABC as commentators again on election night in November of 1968. They did not debate for their appearances nor did they appear together; in separate rooms, each man was brought on for individual commentaries as the evening progressed. They were never to see one another or speak to one another again. Except through their lawyers.

Howard K. Smith: Tonight, the Democratic ticket is complete, and now the tickets of the two major parties of the United States are complete, the battle lines are drawn. I would like to ask our guest commentators to comment on those two tickets. Our commentators, of course, are Gore Vidal, author, playwright, a noted liberal, and William Buckley, editor, one-time New York mayoral candidate, a noted conservative. You are first tonight, Mr. Buckley. Can you compare or comment on these two tickets that will face one another in November?

William F. Buckley Jr.: Sure. I think what I'd like to say most about the Democratic ticket is the occurrence today to which I attack, attach, the greatest significance, which is the statement by Senator McCarthy that he will refuse to endorse that ticket. Under certain circumstances I don't think that would mean very much. We have had political quarrels in the past after a resolution of which an individual says, "I refuse to go along," for whatever reason. But the reason I think it is especially important here today is because there is a congruity between this show of personal independence and a sense which I think has been encouraged among certain Democrats, largely younger Democrats, of total independence from any kind of authority, from any kind of identification with the decisions of a majority within their own party. Now, I understand very well the role of private moral authority. An individual should decide for himself whether he will back any ticket or not. But it is moral philosophers, I think, rather than public men who primarily illustrate that particular imperative. So I predict that Senator McCarthy's refusal to go along is going to have a disintegrative effect not merely on the Democratic Party, which as a Republican doesn't concern me greatly, but also on the whole notion of what it is that you need to keep civic union working.

Howard K. Smith: Mr. Vidal, what do you think about that McCarthy statement? Do you think that it's as serious as that, too? Is the Democratic Party for the first time going to have a fight and not unite after the fight?

Gore Vidal: I think it is quite serious. I don't see the party uniting as it was, say, four years ago. Which that was a rather unusual victory, a rather unusual consensus, as Lyndon Johnson would say. I'm not quite sure to the extent that Senator McCarthy will defect. I talked to him this afternoon, as a matter of fact, about half an hour. His mood was extraordinarily serene and untroubled. I think he was waiting to see, really, how Hubert Humphrey will behave about the war, what the campaign will look like. Meanwhile, he said that he would campaign vigorously for certain senators, on the grounds that it was — after all, it was the Roman senate that had saved that republic, so maybe this senate will save our republic. I think there will be a fourth party movement, in a sense balancing on the left what George Wallace is doing on the right. I think this is apt to come about in the next few weeks. I think there may be even a tendency to try and put Senator McCarthy's name on a fourth party ballot line in at least 25 states.

Howard K. Smith: Do you think he would agree?

Vidal: His attitude is wherever he could take himself off legally he would feel obligated to do so. He is still a member of the Democratic Party. Where he was not obligated to take it off by law there is nothing that he could do about it. That means that you could in effect put his name up or anybody's name up. In certain states, whether the man himself wants to run or not is irrelevant. I see a great split occurring. And I would agree with Mr. Buckley to this extent, that I am almost absolutely convinced that Richard Nixon will win the election.

Howard K. Smith: Can you compare the tickets? We know that the Democrats now are in a weak position. Can you now compare the individuals as campaigners, Humphrey and Nixon? Can you comment on that, Mr. Buckley?

Buckley: I think they are both vigorous campaigners. I think that Mr. Humphrey suffers from certain of the disadvantages Mr. Nixon suffered under in 1960, namely the inevitable number two-ness of the image considering the fact that he continues to be an active vice president. It would seem to be in that connection that Mr. Humphrey would have very little to lose but a considerable amount to gain if he were to resign as vice president under grounds of the explicit incompatibility of the two assignments. In point of fact I don't see why that isn't accepted as a matter of national protocol that on the one hand it is impossible to be totally subservient, as practice requires you to be to a president whom you serve as vice president. On the other hand, to strike out and establish an independent image of your own, a kind that you are attempting to sell to the body of the people. So he has this disadvantage. Mr. Nixon doesn't have that disadvantage at this point. He is proceeding I think surely, optimistically, not in my judgment taking advantage of any of the major lesions of the Democratic Party. Under the circumstances, I think, that indirectly, he comes out at this moment very strong.

Howard K. Smith: People say quite often, and I think they may be right, that this election may not be decided by the circumstances we see now. They may be decided by events in the world that happen between now and November. Can you see any events, Mr. Vidal, that would change this trend you are talking about that Nixon is likely to win?

Vidal: I think if there were suddenly some extraordinary good news from Southeast Asia such as a peace treaty or complete cooling off of the war which might then get back the peace party or parties which would fragment off, I think that would be very helpful to the Democratic candidate. Conversely, if there is a great deal of any more trouble in the cities of the sort that we've seen here in Chicago, I think that this will probably act against the Democrats and will be extremely useful to the Republicans. All they have to do is sit by and let the cities blow up and look as though they might be able to handle it. They really have a perfectly splendid year ahead of them.

Howard K. Smith: I was the moderator in the first Kennedy-Nixon debates. I hope there's going to be a debate between these two highly articulate men. Mr. Buckley, you have a way with words. Which of the two do you think would be the better debater [or] handle himself better in the debates?

Buckley: Well, I think that Mr. Humphrey is more mellifluous than Mr. Nixon, but this may not be a time for mellifluity. Mr. Humphrey, you may notice, when he is in jams, is always extending his heart to whoever is in trouble. He is either doing that or dropping bombs on people or at least justifying the doing of that as he does in Vietnam, I think, with some justification. He is, I think, smoother than Mr. Nixon. Mr. Nixon, on the other hand, has I think a policy of gravity which alienates some of the people, but doesn't alienate all the people. On the contrary, there are times when gravity is very much in order. Concerning sheer intellectual competence, I think both of them are highly qualified. Concerning a quality of apprehending and integrating what the movements are in political life, Nixon comes out ahead, and you may discover this if you moderate the next one.

Howard K. Smith: What do you think, Mr. Vidal, about the ability of the two men to handle issues in public in contests with one another?

Vidal: Well, no reflection Mr. Smith upon your first debate, which I remember very well between Kennedy and Nixon, but I think these great debates are absolutely nonsense. The way they are set up there is almost no interchange of ideas, very little, even, of personality. If we remember, everybody decided that Nixon looked rather disagreeable, Kennedy didn't look as young as they'd been told. He looked much solider, he seemed to have a nicer smile. It's too frivolous. There's also the terrible thing about this medium that hardly anyone listens. They sort of get an impression of somebody and they think they figure out just what he's like by seeing him on television. This would mean that you might have the most disastrous man in the country who happened to be a good television performer and he could beat, let us say, Senator Taft, a virtuous man of no great telegenic charm. So all in all, I hate to suddenly come out against the idea of debates in our lives, but the way they are now set up on television, I don't think I'd even bother to watch this one.

Howard K. Smith: You know that we once hypothetically decided how each of our presidents would look in a television debate. We decided George Washington couldn't make it because his plates fit ill and that Thomas Jefferson had shifty eyes and couldn't make it. We finally decided only Warren Harding would have made a presidential impression on television. What qualities then if you don't believe in debates . . . what would you suggest that people judge candidates by?

Vidal: I think we all get very frustrated watching our friend

Mr. [Lawrence] Spivak, a very good man, good journalist. But watching him in these television programs [**Editor's Note:** Vidal is referring to the television program *Meet the Press.*] and you get a politician on the run, you ask question one, you watch him evade, move to question two, what does he mean?, what's his position?, what's he all about? and what happens? They deflect off and they go off into the next question. In other words, there's no follow-up. I'd much rather see two or three sharp journalists who would be allowed to continue a dialogue, let us say, with the candidates right straight through. What do you really think about Vietnam? What do you really think about the American empire? What is your view of the whole? That, I think would be quite fascinating. And give the candidate an hour. I think that'd be much better than two men playing it extremely cool with one another realizing that the first who is totally disagreeable would probably lose.

Howard K. Smith: Mr. Buckley, I'm going to ask you to undertake an exercise of imagination. Suppose Hubert Humphrey asked you in despair, "What is the best line I could take in this campaign? What issues should I make the most of?" What would you suggest?

Buckley: If I were Mr. Humphrey and my assignment were exclusively to try to get him elected, here is what I would say. I would say, "Look, my friend, we live in very mutinous times. We live in an age, and I'm willing to take a part of the responsibility for it, when people wander around pursuing their own private vision irrespective of whether or not it gets in the way of other people. Since most of these civil disobedients are Democrats or to the left of Democrats it is important that they be approachable by somebody whose position on the spectrum is contiguous to theirs." You might say, "Look what would have happened if Barry Goldwater had been elected president in 1964? Can you imagine his having successfully withstood the domestic opposition to the Vietnam War during the past four years?" So Humphrey might say, "How can a Nixon speak to the hippies, speak to the Spocks and the Coughlins?" Nixon, no doubt, would answer, "Well, there is no reason to speak to them, one only emotes to them." But nevertheless, he would have walked off with a very sound and very cogent point, namely it is impossible to leap over that particular spectrum and communicate with the mutinous elements in our society and that this is a good reason for his election.

Howard K. Smith: Mr. Vidal, can you do exactly the same thing in reverse? Suppose Mr. Nixon called you in and said, "I need help and I trust very much your opinion and you know what Democrats think. How can I lure most of them away?"

Vidal: That is an extraordinary assignment, Mr. Smith. It's a fantasy that I wouldn't dare conceive. I would rather take it right back again to what I might talk to Mr. Humphrey about.

Howard K. Smith: All right.

Vidal: And that would be, we've heard here about the disparate and mutinous visions in our society. I'd say, "If you wanted

175

to be president of this country at this moment [then] you're going to have to come forward and stop offering your heart, and you're going to have to stop saying that we must all be joyful, and you're going to have to offer them an alternative vision. And you're going to have to get right down to what are the things that are wrong with the society, about our imperial pretensions, where are they leading us? Why are they so expensive? Why are things going so badly for us? I think if you were honest about that you could pick up the young and the uncommitted who are extremely angry this year." I would say to Mr. Humphrey, "If you want to capture the ghettos, capture the Negroes, then I'd say break up the cities, devise plans. This can be done. These cities are now too large to be properly serviced, properly even to live in, as we've just been discovering here. They must all be rethought. These are fundamental, radical in the true sense — radical comes from the Latin word meaning root — you must go down to the roots of these problems." Finally, I would say, "Look, we are destroying the planet on which we live. We are destroying the water supply. We are destroying the air supply. We are using up the land. We are running out of food. These are the things which must be done to use the land properly, to clean the air, to clean the water. I would keep right down to the basic things instead of a speech here to the Poles, a speech here to the Italians, all the usual calculated, stupid politics that the young are angry, furious with and now disdainful of."

Howard K. Smith: Now, proposing what to do, I think President Johnson observed, is not really hard. We know a great deal about the problems, but getting those things done is an awful problem. Mr. Buckley, how could a man who wanted to be president cause people to think he could get these things through Congress and administered by states and counties and cities and carried out successfully?

Buckley: The answer is he can't and he shouldn't. The principal obligation of a president of a free people is constantly to remind them that they will be happy or not according as by their own efforts or those of their neighbors and those of their friends and those of their neighborhoods they succeed or do not succeed in making progress through life. Any society is doomed to unsuccess if it elects a president and in turn expects [him] to transmute what we live in into a paradise. This is, of course, the principal difference between the Republican and the Democratic Party as I mentioned a while ago, to whit that the Republican Party is more closely united to the notion that the role of government is to make possible the avenues of progress in a cluttered situation but not to make that progress itself. And this I judge to be the supreme responsibility of a man who desires to be president, as I say, of a free as distinguished from an unfree society.

Howard K. Smith: Mr. Vidal, do you agree with that thesis that what a president has to do is not to get the government to do things but to get the government to permit other private bodies to do things?

Vidal: No, I think that the government must in many ways be even the employer of last resort. Without some kind of strong central pushing you would never have integrated the schools. There probably wouldn't be a forest left in the United States. People at the local level have a great tendency to simply do things that will make a great deal of money, whether in the long run they are wise things to do or not. I think things like the Pure Drug and Food Act and the Department of Interior, these are all useful things that the government does. However, there has been a great malaise in the country about the federal government. After all, it is rather unwieldy. It is very good at collecting money and rather bad at dispersing services. In a sense it's the whole point of black power, which is simply [that] you have more autonomy, and that means economic autonomy, at the local level, at the neighborhood, that you decide what sort of community you want to live in and the federal government to the extent it can bring that desire into being, realize it, and to that extent the president must leave the government itself as a guide. You must keep a balance between locality and the center of a society.

Howard K. Smith: Mr. Buckley, Mr. Vidal said he couldn't make that act of imagination whereby he would advise former Vice President Nixon what to do to win. Suppose you had that job thrust on you. What would you suggest doing?

Buckley: Well, I think I would begin by stressing what I said a moment ago, namely the solemn obligation of a president to say, "Don't elect me in lieu of yourselves, in lieu of your religion, your preachers, your teachers, the rest of it, your family because I can't perform all those services for you nor should I attempt to do so." One more thing I think Mr. Nixon ought as a result of the special historical circumstances to try to do is to attempt to show that the moral arrogance which characterizes most of the dissenting units in our society today are going to make democracy impossible. That is to say, if everyone believes, for instance, that the right of assembly is also the right to bring his protest right through police lines right into the heart of an amphitheater that is trying to transact political business, then necessarily in a society that seeks such order as Mr. Kennedy was talking about in this posthumous film, [**Editor's Note:** A reference to a brief film about Bobby Kennedy shown at the Democratic Convention], such a society is simply not going to succeed. Under the circumstances Mr. Nixon has that duty to remind people what it is that keeps a society together. Namely a disposition by the minority to grant to the majority certain civil authority, not moral authority, but civil authority, and I think that if he successfully formulated that he would find an enormous response not merely by Republicans but also by Democrats who want to continue in a free society and know how much is at stake.

Howard K. Smith: We make our political editors make forecasts about what's going to happen. May I ask each of you — Mr. Vidal has answered this — but may I ask each of you to tell me what do you think is going to happen in November? Is someone going to win — big, or little? Or is it going to be an unimpressive victory? First, Mr. Buckley.

Buckley: I think Mr. Nixon will win and that but for Wallace he would win impressively.

Howard K. Smith: Mr. Vidal.

Vidal: I think that Nixon will win. I think that we will also see the rise of a permanent fourth party and that this will continue to be active in our affairs for some time because the two major parties are to my mind bankrupt.

Howard K. Smith: Thank you very much, gentlemen. We're going to have acceptance speeches later tonight. I wish you were here to comment on them, but, if not, we'll try to do our best.

William F. Buckley Jr. (1925-2008)

The son of a millionaire oil tycoon, Bill Buckley came to
public notice in 1951 with his book *God and Man at Yale* in
which he scathingly indicted the Eastern liberal establishment
for what he felt was their utter control of academia at Ivy
League schools. He founded a magazine in 1955 aimed at
the nascent conservative movement, *National Review,* which
became the Holy Writ of the American right-wing. In 1966
Buckley, who had an odd telegenic appeal that viewers
found captivating, began the long-running television show,
Firing Line, where Buckley debated issues of the day with a
variety of guests of all political persuasions. (It was a source
of disagreement between Buckley and Vidal as to whether
Vidal had ever been invited on *Firing Line.*) Buckley's ideal
presidential candidate was elected in 1980, Ronald Reagan,
who claimed *National Review* was his favorite periodical.
Buckley, like his nemesis Mr. Vidal, was an indefatigable
worker and authored over 50 books. Although he had seen
his conservative vision rise to the forefront of American
politics, he died deeply unhappy at what he felt was the
anti-intellectual pendulum swing within the right-wing.

Gore Vidal (1925-2012)

Gore Vidal shocked the literary world in 1946 when at the tender age of 21 he published his first novel, the critically-acclaimed *Williwaw*, based on his experience in the Aleutian Islands during World War II. The son of a groundbreaking aviator (Eugene Vidal) who was Director of Air Commerce in the Roosevelt Administration and socialite Nina Gore, who was the daughter of Oklahoma Senator Thomas Pryor Gore, Vidal showed brilliance at an early age. After his first two novels, he published *City and the Pillar* in 1948, which scandalized readers and critics with its realistic depiction of a homosexual relationship that did not suggest homo-sexuality as deviant behavior. Vidal was lured to Hollywood as a screenwriter, where he amassed enough money to continue with his novels and to pursue liberal politics in essays that were noted for their eloquence, sharp observa-tions, and elegant prose. Handsome and refined, Vidal was perfect for the new medium of television and found himself welcomed as a witty talk show guest and panelist on game shows. In 1968 Vidal published the controversial *Myra Breckinridge*, about a conniving transsexual whose escapades provided a sexually-awakening America with some delicious-ly naughty reading. It was an enormous bestseller despite the denouncements from more conservative quarters. After proving himself a master of the essay, play, screenplay, and novel, Vidal found even greater success with a succession of historical novels, *Burr, Lincoln, Julian, 1896,* and many others. Although his views were considered too radical by many, his observations and criticisms of American society never failed to engross (and enrage) readers the world over. He never quite got over his resentments against Mr. Buckley. When Buckley died and he was asked for a comment he replied, "R.I.P. WFB — in hell."

Howard K. Smith (1914-2002)

A Rhodes scholar who studied German and journalism, a
young Howard K. Smith became an earnest and talented
junior reporter for the United Press and then *The New York
Times*. In 1940 he was sent to Germany and was hired by
Edward R. Murrow of CBS radio and became one of
"Murrow's Boys" and a familiar voice to Americans from his
radio broadcasts. He was kicked out of Nazi Germany for
refusing to add propaganda to his broadcasts. After the war,
he continued his work in radio and then in the new medium
of television. He jumped from CBS to ABC after a row with
CBS head William Paley and became a staple of the underdog
network. In 1969 he became co-anchor of the evening news,
a position he held for 10 years. Smith moderated the first of
the Nixon-Kennedy debates, which undoubtedly prepared
him for the coal and sulphur of the Buckley-Vidal debates of
1968.

Suggested Reading

Smiling Through the Apocalypse: Esquire's History of the Sixties (out-of-print, originally published by The McCall Publishing Company, New York)

This anthology is the one place that readers can find the uncensored 1969 *Esquire* articles, "On Experiencing Gore Vidal" by William Buckley and "A Distasteful Encounter with William Buckley" by Gore Vidal (there is, of course, the Internet). As heated as the debates were at times, both Buckley and Vidal gave full vent to their mutual antipathy in the *Esquire* articles, which led, ultimately, to a circus of lawsuits that cost both men, both emotionally and monetarily. *Esquire* settled out of court with Buckley, and one of the terms was that Buckley had to give permission before *Esquire* (or anyone else for that matter) could ever reprint Vidal's article. That power of denial is still ongoing and Buckley's heir, his son Christopher, has disallowed "A Distasteful Encounter with William Buckley" from being republished. Thus, this out-of-print volume remains the only source for the articles outside hunting down the original 1969 *Esquire* issues. Amazon.com and other sources carry the title at not unreasonable prices.

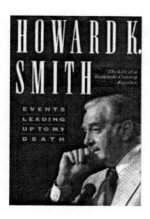

Events Leading Up to My Death: The Life of a Twentieth Century Reporter (out-of-print, originally published by St. Martin's Press, New York)

Also out-of-print but readily available on Amazon.com and other retailers, Howard K. Smith's *Events Leading Up to My Death* is a page-turner of a biography of a man who led at least as fascinating a life as Mr. Buckley and Mr. Vidal. He also writes amusingly about the tete-a-tete between Buckley and Vidal and provides a few *I-was-there* details no one else has.

Other Books You Might Enjoy from Devault-Graves Digital Editions

Nonfiction

Do You Sleep in the Nude? by Rex Reed

People Are Crazy Here by Rex Reed

Conversations in the Raw by Rex Reed

Valentines & Vitriol by Rex Reed

Weegee: The Autobiography

Louise Brooks, Frank Zappa, & Other Charmers & Dreamers by Tom Graves

Crossroads: The Life and Afterlife of Blues Legend Robert Johnson by Tom Graves

Sun Records: An Oral History by John Floyd

Graceland Too Revisited (photography) by Darrin Devault and Tom Graves

Fiction

Three Early Stories by J.D. Salinger

Big Sur by Jack Kerouac

Maggie Cassidy by Jack Kerouac

Tristessa by Jack Kerouac

CPSIA information can be obtained
at www.ICGtesting.com
Printed in the USA
LVOW11s1217031116
511447LV00002BA/205/P